WHY WE WRITE ABOUT OURSELVES

Leslie Bohm Photography

MEREDITH MARAN published her first memoir at age nineteen and has since written several memoirs and narrative nonfiction books including *Why We Write*, *My Lie*, and *Class Dismissed*, as well as the 2012 novel *A Theory of Small Earthquakes*. She writes essays and book reviews for newspapers and magazines including *People*, *Salon.com*, the *Boston Globe*, and the *Los Angeles Times*. She lives in Silver Lake, Los Angeles, and on Twitter at @meredithmaran.

Why We Write About Ourselves

Twenty Memoirists on Why They
Expose Themselves (and Others)
in the Name of Literature

Edited by Meredith Maran

A PLUME BOOK

PLUME
An imprint of Penguin Random House LLC
375 Hudson Street
New York, New York 10014
penguin.com

P REGISTERED TRADEMARK—MARCA REGISTRADA

LIBRARY OF CONGRESS CATALOGING-IN-PUBLICATION DATA
   Why we write about ourselves : twenty memoirists on why they expose themselves
(and others) in the name of literature / edited by Meredith Maran.
      pages cm
   ISBN 978-0-14-218197-3 (paperback)
   1. Autobiography—Authorship. 2. Biography as a literary form. I. Maran, Meredith,
editor.
   PE1479.A88W48 2016
   808.06'692—dc23   2015015830

Printed in the United States of America
10 9 8 7 6 5 4 3 2 1

Set in Adobe Caslon Pro
Designed by Eve L. Kirch

For those who read memoirs and those who write memoirs,
and for those who wish we wouldn't.
We're all just looking for truth, aren't we.

Contents

Acknowledgments

Oh, Becky Cole. Becky Cole! What's not to love about an editor who starts her edit letter, "Do you have five minutes? Then you can probably make the requested changes in the ms. Golly, it's good." Thank you, Becky, for keeping both of us laughing even when certain unnamed memoirists (not one of whom appears in this book) proved to be kind of, well, *difficult*, causing us to wonder whether we could get away with, say, thirteen or fourteen contributors instead of twenty.

Linda Loewenthal, you're such a good person, it's hard to believe you're an agent. You're more like a spirit guide. A spirit guide who's also a hardass negotiator and brilliant thinker and editor and book-doula and muse and, most of all, an indefatigable, unflagging, loving literary companion. Thank you. I love you.

For time, space, and profound nourishment: a thousand picnic basketsful of thanks to the artists' colonies MacDowell,

Yaddo, the Mesa Refuge, Ragdale, the Virginia Center for the Creative Arts, and the Mabel Dodge Luhan House.

Booksellers and independent bookstore owners: I hope everyone who buys this book will buy it from you.

To my friends and family: Thank you for holding me up, at all times, no matter what.

Introduction

I've given my memoirs far more thought than any of my marriages. You can't divorce a book.

—Gloria Swanson

～〜つ

Gloria's right. You can't divorce a memoir. But, as the twenty successful authors in this book attest, you can (and some do) divorce, disown, de-friend, or defame a memoirist. If you want to ruin your life and/or others', there's really no more sure-fire method than writing a true-life tale according to you.

Why, then, do so many authors risk public, private, and/or professional excoriation for the dubious pleasure of writing about themselves? What is it about sharing one's deepest thoughts, feelings, and experiences with others that makes it worth the mayhem and mishegas?

Without demand, of course, there would be no supply. So we must also ask why we *read* memoirs. For centuries, readers, reviewers, and social commentators have been gobbling up first-person narratives, all the while diagnosing the books' authors with attention-seeking disorders. Is the urge to read memoirs the same urge that makes us peek into strangers' undraped windows at night—not *just* because we're nosy, but to learn something from how other people live, in order to live better lives ourselves?

Whatever the reasons for our attachment to memoir, it's a phenomenon that's unlikely to go away anytime soon. The genre has been around since St. Augustine wrote his thirteen-volume *Confessions* around A.D. 400. In one form or another, memoir lives on today—in the journal entry, blog, confessional e-mail, or Facebook post you wrote an hour ago. Forgive us, Descartes; today's philosophy of existence might best be expressed thusly: "I overshare, therefore I am."

⁓

People who love memoirs claim that the telling of the true-life story is the contemporary incantation of oral history, an invaluable contribution to the enlightenment, the collective consciousness, perhaps even the evolution of the species.

People who don't love memoirs say the genre is a scourge upon the human race, a playing field upon which attention-craving, sensationalistic, crass, and craven narcissists head-butt and navel-gaze their way to the bestseller lists.

Between the covers of this book, twenty very different memoirists share their very different reasons for doing what they do and their sometimes different, sometimes overlapping approaches to the controversies that surround the genre.

"I'm always asking myself if material I have from my own life would be best used in a novel or a memoir or a short story or an essay," says Cheryl Strayed. "I was moved to write *Wild* as a memoir because I thought that was the best way to tell that particular story."

"I actually never intended to publish a book," says Ishmael Beah, whose bestselling *A Long Way Gone* describes his life as a twelve-year-old soldier in Sierra Leone. "Writing [became] for me a way to prove my existence."

"Some of us are the designated rememberers," *The Death of Santini* author Pat Conroy told me. "That's why memoir interests us—because we're the ones who pass the stories."

"I have never written memoir by choice," says Edwidge Danticat, author of *Brother, I'm Dying*. "Each time I write memoir, in short or long form, something happens that compels me to do it—something that feels pressing and urgent, something that there is no other way to express."

How does memoir writing differ from journal keeping? Should a memoir be a work of art, produced for the benefit of the reader—or a cathartic writing experience for the benefit of the author?

"People want to believe that a memoirist has simply opened a vein and bled on the page," according to Ayelet Waldman. "That's a diary. A diary can be emotionally satisfying, it can be great therapy, but it's not necessarily good writing."

"A memoir is not simply stringing together the five or ten good stories you've been telling about your wacky childhood for your whole life," Nick Flynn says.

But A. M. Homes says she wrote a memoir about her adoption "to organize the information and the experience—to put it in a container, if only to set the container aside for a while."

When I asked the writers about the morality of memoir—whether memoirists are obligated to protect the privacy of the loved (and not-loved) ones in their lives—emotions ran high.

Sue Monk Kidd said that writing memoir is "a dance between being true to my need to write authentically and my responsibility to those around me not to cross over into their private hearts and extract something that doesn't belong to me."

Edmund White said, "Memoir should be extremely honest and personal. It should show the author for who he is, warts and all . . . A memoirist's contract with the reader is that you're telling the truth and nothing but the truth. That requires telling everything there is to say about everyone involved."

"What I worried about most, writing the memoir," said Kate Christensen, "was offending people or causing anyone pain. I'm used to writing about invented characters. Writing about real people was a huge stretch—a leap into new territory."

"At first I was worried that my book would be really exploitive," Anne Lamott said. "But then my editor said, 'It won't be exploitive if you don't exploit anyone.'"

Whatever your thoughts and feelings about this provocative, evocative genre, whether you're a producer or a consumer of memoir, or neither, or both, I hope you'll benefit from the literary, emotional, psychological, and moral self-examination that's on display in these pages.

In their own books, the memoirists included here bare all. In *this* book, they bare all about baring all, excavating the personal and professional agonies and ecstasies, moral conundrums, and psychological battles that come with the job.

—Meredith Maran

Why We Write
About Ourselves

CHAPTER ONE

Ishmael Beah

There were all kinds of stories told about the war that made it sound as if it was happening in a faraway and different land. It wasn't until refugees started passing through our town that we began to see that it was actually taking place in our country.

—Opening, *A Long Way Gone*, 2007

In 1993, when Ishmael Beah was twelve years old, antigovernment soldiers invaded his village of Mogbwemo, Sierra Leone. Along with many other boys, he fled the village, spent months wandering the countryside, and was then conscripted into the government army at age thirteen. In 1996, after witnessing and committing unthinkable acts of war, Ishmael was rescued by UNICEF, which helped him with his rehabilitation and reinsertion into normal life. He was later adopted by an American woman, Laura Simms, and found a home and a school—the United Nations International School—in New York City.

From there Ishmael made his way to Oberlin College, where he studied political science and took some creative writing courses with the novelist Dan Chaon. By the time he graduated in 2004, Ishmael had a draft of the memoir that would become *A Long Way Gone*, his account of his years as a child soldier.

The book was an immediate hit; it has since sold more than 1.5 million copies. But its publication was not without controversy. In early 2009, Rupert Murdoch's *Australian* investigated Ishmael's story and said that his account was exaggerated. The paper claimed that the attack on Ishmael's village had happened in 1995, not 1993 as described in *A Long Way Gone*. Since Ishmael had been rescued by UNICEF in 1996, the *Australian* claimed, he'd been a child soldier for months, not years.

Three days after the article appeared, Ishmael published a rebuttal, saying, "I am right about my story. This is not something one gets wrong . . . Sad to say, my story is all true."

Ishmael's publisher, Sarah Crichton at Farrar, Straus and Giroux, stood firmly behind him. His adoptive mother said, "I knew this was not fraudulent. The last thing that Ishmael would want is to lie about what he cannot forget."

For Ishmael, being accused of lying is small potatoes, compared to living with those memories.

"If I choose to feel guilty for what I have done, I will want to be dead myself," he has said. "I live knowing that I have been given a second life, and I just try to have fun, and be happy and live it the best I can."

The Vitals

Birthday: November 23, 1980

Born and raised: Born in Mattru Jong and raised in Mogbwemo, Bonthe District, Sierra Leone

Home now: New York, New York

Family: Married to Priscillia Kounkou Hoveyda; one daughter

Schooling: United Nations International School; Oberlin College, BA in political science

Day job: Author and activist; volunteer for UNICEF and Human Rights Watch

Notable notes:
- *A Long Way Gone* was selected as the second title featured in Starbucks' Book Break program.
- Ishmael was nominated for a Quill Award for Debut Author of the Year; *Time* named *A Long Way Gone* one of its Top 10 Nonfiction Books of 2007.
- In an interview with his Oberlin College mentor, Dan Chaon, Ishmael said, "When you're writing you feel like there are probably other forces at work, like the words are just coming out of you. They're very sweet moments, but they don't last very long."

Twitter: @IshmaelBeah

Website: www.ishmaelbeah.com

The Collected Works

Memoir

A Long Way Gone, 2007

Novel

Radiance of Tomorrow, 2014

Ishmael Beah

Why I write about myself

I do not consider myself a memoirist. I consider myself a writer who happened to be introduced as a writer to the world through a memoir, a nonfictional book. I actually never intended to publish a book.

Prior to making the commitment to write my memoir, writing had become for me a way to prove my existence. Apart from my passport, I had no physical objects or documentation to do so.

I remember when I began applying to schools in the United States. I was asked to provide a report card. "I don't have one," I would say. Often the response was "Well, everyone has a report card." I would chuckle and correct them. "I'm from Sierra Leone, and I don't have one."

When I started high school in New York, I wrote an essay titled "Why I Do Not Have a Report Card." I got a glimpse then that my core reason for writing would be to expose people to certain realities and hope to deepen their understanding of the other, of places that may seem far away.

A sense of urgency made me do it

The story of *A Long Way Gone* was the first story I needed to tell with urgency. There were other stories within me, but this one possessed me.

Writing it also came out of several frustrations. I felt the need to correct the way my people and my country were portrayed. Each time I said to someone that I was from Sierra Leone, they responded by telling me about the horrors of the civil war, as though it had always been that way and as if war was the only identity of my country. There was no context, and more important, no human context, in the way my people were presented. Here I was, a young man living away from home, carrying a splinter of the very story that was misrepresented. So I had to do something about it, using my small part of a much larger story.

Writing as if each book might be my last

Whether I am writing nonfiction or fiction, I always write about things that are meaningful to me—situations that speak to my being. I approach each piece of writing, whether it's a short story, a book, or a novel, as though it were the first and last story I will write.

There was risk involved

I worried that people wouldn't want to read my memoir because their initial response to the subject matter was only a reaction to the violence, the kind they hear or read about, without the human context and framework. That framework has the power to make a person understand that there is nowhere in the world where people will choose violence if they have other viable ways of living.

My aspiration was to show how everyone is capable of violence if you happen to find yourself in circumstances that propel you toward violence as a way to live. I wanted to show that no one can decide ahead of time whether you will embrace violence or not until you are in a certain situation.

I very much wanted to show the realities of war. At the same time, I was overwhelmed by the need to be careful not to write something that could be mistaken as an endorsement or a celebration of violence.

I was fueled by the importance of putting the human face on war, the worst kind of war, and showing the strength of human beings to outlive life's worst circumstances. I wanted to show that beauty and hope can exist even when there is no reason for hope, even when it seems all has been lost.

Protecting the innocent

For those people in my memoir who were alive and I could find, I explained to them what I was embarking on and that I would present them from my point of view. Those who weren't comfortable, I used only their first names.

As to my own privacy, I just wrote from how I thought about things as a child, in sort of a matter-of-fact way and unapologetically. I had to return to how I felt about things as a child, as a boy, not as the young man I had become by the time I wrote the book.

I knew, though, from the beginning, that I wouldn't share everything. It isn't possible to write about everything, and some things I needed to keep for my family and myself—the deepest intimacies of my emotions and experiences. My desire was to take moments of my life to make a point, and that is what I did.

I feel satisfied that I succeeded in getting across what war does to human beings and the possibility of recovering. Those who haven't been in war can never truly understand it, but I made them come as close as possible to that reality.

Being called a liar is not pleasant

When certain people in the media accused me of making up parts of my story and exaggerating the length of my time as a soldier, it was frustrating and annoying to argue with them about it. Those "reporters" weren't in my country during the war and had very little understanding of what happened and very little understanding of war in general. I found their claims ridiculous and unfounded and hence they never went anywhere. I stand fully by what I wrote.

When I wrote the memoir, I relied on the best of my memories and I took out anything I doubted. My memoir was fact-checked. Memoirs don't just get published. Excerpts from my book were published in *The New York Times Magazine* before the book was released, and the magazine did its own fact-checking.

So when certain people started with their nonsense I just laughed. I wasn't a journalist who inserted himself in war to experience it and therefore had notepads, cameras, and the like to record what happened. Unfortunately, they approached my story from that angle, as if I had cameras and notepads with me the whole time.

The media were caught up with this idea of the singular truth about the war in my country. Well, any sensible person would know that when several people experience the same event, they remember different aspects of that event. Still, all of their recollections would be truthful to what occurred. The guy standing with his back to me when I was shooting, as I was during the war, would have a very different telling of that event than mine. And yet both stories would be true to that experience.

Lying is not right, either

The question of morality arises in a memoir only if the writer deliberately tells a story of deceit or chooses to blatantly portray people through outright lies for purposes of slander and sensation. It's also immoral for the narrator to paint him- or herself in a saintly light.

Of course, when you write about people, you always write your version of the truth about them. You write about how you see them, not how they view themselves. Otherwise they would be the authors.

As a writer, with any story, whether it's fiction or nonfiction, you make choices to show certain aspects of your characters to make a point or to introduce an idea or to hint at what you want your readers to understand.

Ishmael Beah's Wisdom for Memoir Writers

- Do not aspire to be a memoirist. Rather, seek to write your truth without thinking about the readers or publication. If you do that, you have already started writing someone else's story.

- Be completely open to discovering things about yourself as you delve into your memories. You'll be surprised at what your mind reveals to you about who you are.

- Never try to please those you write about. You will not succeed and will certainly ruin your story.

CHAPTER TWO

Kate Christensen

Often, whenever I come up against anything painful or difficult, my mind escapes to food. I am sure I am far from alone in this. Even if I'm too upset to eat, just the thought of a grilled cheese sandwich and a bowl of tomato soup is warm and cozy and savory and comforting.

—Opening, *Blue Plate Special*, 2013

Kate Christensen writes novels, memoirs, magazine features, essays, reviews, and a blog. She narrates some of her novels in the voices of men; others as women. Her memoir *Blue Plate Special* began as an ode to food and evolved into an exposé of her violent father and her childhood sexual assault. She's an unrepentant sensualist whose love story with her twenty-years-younger boyfriend—and his family's New Hampshire farmhouse; the beautiful meals they cook and the beautiful wine they drink in the 1860s house they remodeled together in Portland, Maine; and their winter walks through the woods with their beloved dog, Dingo—runs through her writings like an upbeat background hum.

Kate Christensen can write a character who will make you yell at the book in your hand and she can write a plate of pasta puttanesca that will make you want to take a bite of the page. Her books and her life are a celebration of edible, emotional, quotidian joy. And they are the redemption story of a woman who slept with the wrong men, drank too many drinks, and lived a whole lot of pain.

Lucky us: we're the beneficiaries of all of it.

THE VITALS

Birthday: August 22, 1962

Born and raised: Berkeley, California

Home now: Portland, Maine

Family: Boyfriend, Brendan

Schooling: Reed College; Iowa Writers' Workshop

Day job: Nope

Notable notes:
- In 2008, Kate won the PEN/Faulkner Award for her novel *The Great Man*.
- "Just as the ingredients at hand can dictate a dish," Kate says, "the characters who arise in my imagination and are set in motion at the beginning of a novel can dictate its plot, tone, and themes."
- Kate writes about food and drink for many national publications, including *Vogue* and *Food & Wine*.

Facebook: https://www.facebook.com/kate.christensen.39?fref=ts

Twitter: @aquavita

Website/blog: https://katechristensen.wordpress.com

THE COLLECTED WORKS

Novels

In the Drink, 1999

Jeremy Thrane, 2001

The Epicure's Lament, 2004

The Great Man, 2007

Trouble, 2009

The Astral, 2011

Nonfiction

Blue Plate Special, 2013

How to Cook a Moose, 2015

Essays, Columns, Reviews (Partial Listing)

The New York Times Book Review

O, The Oprah Magazine

The Wall Street Journal

Elle

Bookforum

Vogue

Cherry Bombe

Food & Wine

Kate Christensen

Why I write about myself

My reasons for writing memoir and fiction are the same. I'm hoping to give my readers connection, comfort, reassurance, and, of course, entertainment.

I've been a "self-chronicler" from a very early age, and I've always done that kind of writing alongside writing fiction. When I was seven or eight I was always writing made-up stories, and I also kept diaries. This journal keeping intensified when I was sixteen, as it did for many of us. It hit a peak in my midtwenties, then tapered off for a number of years until I stopped. I haven't kept a journal since my midthirties.

All this writing about my own life as it happened—
hundreds if not thousands of pages through the years—is remarkable chiefly for its bulk. When I can bear to revisit this
outpouring, I'm struck by how analytical I was able to be about
my predicaments and struggles while remaining helpless to
change anything about any of them.

In hindsight, I think my journal keeping was a colossal exercise in honing and developing my own point of view. What it
wasn't was an agent of self-improvement or a catalyst for
change. Keeping journals wasn't therapeutic. It didn't cause or
encourage me to better my lot. I practiced a kind of mindful
exegesis of daily life, including the vicissitudes of my mostly
problematic sexual and romantic relationships and friendships
and family ties.

I poured out my fears; laid out my plans, hopes, and dreams;
and was unrelenting, unsparing, in my self-loathing chroni-
clings of my own failings. All this navel-gazing is virtually
unreadable now—at least it is to me. I wrote things as they
were, and I stayed stuck. It's frustrating to read them for that
reason. I want to yell, "Get out of there! Quit that job! Leave
that guy! Get a new apartment! Speak up!" It's a bit like watch-
ing a horror movie and wishing you could tell the girl not to go
into the abandoned house alone at night, but of course she does
it anyway.

Almost despite myself, while I was writing so feverishly all
those decades, I was improving. Not my life, but my writing. I
was creating a voice, an "I"—as well as practicing a writerly
detachment from emotion—an ability to record and relay extreme states in dispassionate, clean prose. This served me well
when I began writing novels for real. Looking back on all that

journal keeping, I see it now as a writerly form of finger exercises—études and scales for the aspiring novelist.

I had a parallel passion, also begun at a young age: reading the published diaries, journals, autobiographies, and biographies of famous people. I was enthralled by anyone else's existence. I was hooked on the things that made a life both singular and universal. I loved reading about both men and women, but the lives of remarkable women gave me an added thrill, because they made me feel as if I had a ringside seat to what I might accomplish someday if I paid attention to the gritty courage of Harriet Tubman, the determination of invincible Louisa May Alcott, the passion and intelligence of Anne Frank. I loved and read them all—Helen Keller and Anne Sullivan, Susan B. Anthony, Florence Nightingale, Eleanor Roosevelt—every biography I could get my mitts on as a kid, and on into my adult years, too.

Food writing is life writing

When I was in my late twenties, living in the proverbial East Village rat hole, always broke and always hungover, and insomniacal with anxiety about the future, nothing was more comforting to me than the intersection of food, life, and language. This is how I discovered, and became obsessed with, M. F. K. Fisher and her brilliant chronicles of a life in food. She was my gateway drug to the "foodoir," as I call it—the writings of people as diverse as Laurie Colwin and Nicolas Freeling, who wrote books about life through the prism of food.

Write memoir or hide. You can't do both

Just as reading novels made me want to write them, reading food memoirs made me want to write one myself. But I understood instinctively that I had to wait until my life had a story, an arc, a shape that would lend itself to this sort of enterprise. From my late twenties on, I intended to write a food book as soon as I was ready. Meanwhile, I wrote novels and taught myself to cook and went out to as many restaurants of every kind as I could, at home in New York and on my travels with my then husband. I immersed myself in food and writing and waited for the intersection of the two to happen. During that time, I was wildly unhappy, lonely, and angry, and I was suppressing these things to try to stay in my untenable marriage. It's impossible to write about yourself when you're hiding.

As my fiftieth birthday approached, I recognized that I had become, against all odds, settled, happy, and fulfilled. This hadn't happened by accident. I had made it happen by making difficult choices that led me to it. With much grief and a sense of dark failure, I'd left my marriage. Seven months later, I fell in love with a man twenty years younger than I was but in every other way my perfect match and soul mate. I found myself blessed with a circle of trustworthy, amazing friends. My family had gradually reintegrated after many years of rifts and sorrows.

With Brendan, I left New York and traveled around the world, staying in his family's empty farmhouse in the White Mountains as a home base. We wound up buying a house of our own in Portland, Maine, in 2011. In the months before I turned fifty, I felt immense relief, as if I had come through trials and dangers and, with difficulty and perseverance, landed in a calm, happy, safe, stable life with a man I adored and friends I trusted and the work life I had always striven for. It felt like a happy ending to my long and protracted youth.

And then, suddenly, the itch to write about my own life came back with a vengeance. This time, though, I wanted to write for a readership. I didn't feel the need anymore for private analysis or inchoate ramblings. I wanted to offer artfully shaped essays to readers. I wanted to connect with readers in the course of figuring out, in writing, how my own life was both singular and universal. Above all, I wanted to offer comfort to people who were going through what I'd just come through—years of loneliness.

Writing the memoir was excruciatingly hard—harder than my novels, even. It didn't feel self-indulgent or like wallowing at all. Sometimes it felt like trying to carve a big rough piece of stone with a dull penknife.

What makes it all worth it is hearing from a reader who took some solace from my book. When that happens, I'm so happy.

Writing the foodoir

In the winter of 2011, just after Brendan and I moved to Portland, Maine, I started a blog about food, which quickly became about my own life as well, both the present and the past. And it grew into a food memoir. In writing it, I wanted to repay the debt of comfort and reassurance I felt I owed M. F. K. Fisher and Laurie Colwin. I wrote it for insomniacs at three in the morning who were wondering how they'd get through the next day. And I wrote it for my past self, that girl who promised herself she'd write a book someday.

My relationship with food has been anything but smooth. In addition to pleasure and joy, I've gone through eating disorders, weight swings, hunger, gluttony, alcohol abuse, poverty, and manic loss of appetite. So the memoir had to delve into the darkness. I wanted to lay it all bare as truthfully as I could without being overly analytical. I wanted to show my life in all its messy complexity, its many ups and downs, without trying to codify or label anything. To someone as habitually overly analytical as I've always been, it wasn't easy. But I think the book I wrote is far more visceral than cerebral, as a foodoir should be.

The "I's" have it

Strangely, I don't feel that writing fiction and writing memoir are altogether so different at their core.

The "I" of *Blue Plate Special* and the "I's" of *In the Drink* and *The Epicure's Lament* are all me, and they're all not me. Maybe all writing is autobiographical, to some extent. What makes fiction and nonfiction different, of course, is that in fiction, I'm imagining a life that's parallel to my own but not my own. In nonfiction, I'm recounting, remembering, and shaping a version of my own.

Once the work of memory was done and I had assembled a rough chronology, though, the next step was necessary detachment from the autobiographical "I." That was what allowed me to draw on my novelistic experience and determine what this voice would be, what the shape of her story would be, and how the chronology I'd resurrected would be told. These things are all novelistic questions as well as nonfictional. They're both about storytelling.

A memoir is not a diary

I've written six novels in the past fifteen years. I've had an enormous amount of fun couching my life fictionally in those novels, extrapolating from direct experience as fuel for my imaginative fire. I'm relishing my newfound ability to transcend the self-absorption and artlessness of journal writing into a coherent narrative, to shape the raw material of my life without denying any of its fuckedupness or my own culpability and fallibility. And that ability came directly from many years of writing fiction. The fictional "I" gave rise to the nonfictional one and enabled me to write directly about myself, as a character rather than an unmitigated, diaristic first-person voice.

Blue Plate Special was the most difficult book I've ever written, as well as the easiest. The material was all there. I just had to find the thread, weave it through, and tie it together at the end. No big deal. Ha! It was agony a lot of the time. Ecstasy the rest of the time. Such a roller coaster. I kept vacillating between "I can't do this, it's too hard" and "*God*, this is fun."

The joys and travails of removing the fictional veil

Writing personal essays is a joy, now that I have a solid "I" to work from—and more than a half century of experience to draw on. The older I get, the more interested I am in telling the truth, and the less interested I am in artfulness for its own sake.

Novel writing can be a way of couching, reinventing, transcending—and hiding. Writing personal essays and memoir is a way of revealing myself without that veil. I want to connect. I want to be known. My ego, which was massive when I was younger, isn't what drives me to write anymore. Writing straight into the truth feels like the only thing I want to do now: to connect with the reader, and only that.

What I worried about most, writing the memoir, was offending people or causing anyone pain. I'm used to writing about invented characters. Writing about real people was a huge stretch—a leap into new territory.

I also fear being judged. Oh, I hate being judged. But there's no avoiding it, so I might as well tell the whole truth, lay myself open to it. I'd rather be judged for the truth about myself than be judged for equivocating or trying to protect myself. That said, I still fear (and loathe) being criticized for who I am, misunderstood, found wanting, accused of horrible things.

It's different with my novels. They're not literally me. In writing memoir, I'm opening myself to judgment of my life, not just my writing.

Regrets only

Writing about the rocky years with my mother and the demise of my marriage was excruciating for me. And it was really hard for me to see my mother's initial reaction to the book, which was pained sorrow. One of my primary regrets is that I didn't allow her story to be told all the way through. I dropped that thread in favor of following others, but I think the book would be better, and I think I'd feel better, if I had given an update of her life near the end of the book.

Since I wrote it, my mother has flourished in ways that were only hinted at in the book. I'm so proud of her, and I adore her, and I didn't allow that to come through. Damn.

My friend Rosie Schaap, who wrote the brilliant, beautiful memoir *Drinking with Men*, told me, "The only person who should look like an asshole in your memoir is you." I strove to follow that. I hope I didn't fail too badly.

Do unto others

When I'm writing about the people in my life and I feel myself rowing into dangerous waters, I start typing very slowly, chewing the inside of my cheek, trying to find a delicate passage through it all in which everything is my own perception and nothing is presented as accusation or an ax to grind. I can't have any axes to grind. They're one of the pitfalls of memoir and must be avoided.

Writing about my father was cathartic. He's a complicated person; I loved him blindly and deeply as a girl, and I've had to come to terms with losing him, with his behavior, with the ways in which I am like and not like him. I've been able to let him go, finally. And the rest of my family has become closer.

My mother and sisters and I talked a lot about the past as a result of my writing my memoir. I sent them two different drafts to get their input, and although there's so much more to say, we started a new conversation about "back then" together, in a round robin of e-mails, since we all live in different time zones. I feel closer to them as a result.

In the memoir, and in an *Elle* magazine excerpt from the book, I went public with the truth about the math teacher who molested me in high school. As a result, my school launched an investigation into the rampant sexual abuse that was happening there in the late 1970s and early '80s. I admitted to myself in the course of this process that I had been a victim. And as the truth came out, and everyone who wanted to talk about it on the record had a chance to, thirty-five years later, I resolved the trauma of those years.

I feel free of the past in a way I never dreamed I could be; I also feel as if I understand it. More than a year after the book was written, I have a sense of peace I've never felt before, a feeling of comfort in my own skin.

Self-protection is the enemy of the truth

When I'm writing about myself, I write out of a strong urge *not* to protect myself. When I feel ego or self-justification or defensiveness creeping in or a wish to make myself look better than I was, I squelch it, if I can.

It takes vigilance. Exposing myself is the only way to go, though. If I'd rather wear veils, I should write fiction. I write out of the sure knowledge that the more honest I am, the freer I am, and the freer I am, the happier I am.

Kate Christensen's Wisdom for Memoir Writers

- Don't be afraid of writing into the heart of what you're most afraid of. The story of a life lives in what you would rather not admit or say.

- Memoir writing isn't therapy—it's better than therapy. It opens out your life to the world and lets the world in.

- Finding the universal in the singular, and vice versa, is a challenge and a thrill and, ultimately, a source of tremendous peace.

CHAPTER THREE

Pearl Cleage

I told my daughter over lunch at our favorite hamburger joint that upon my death, which, as far as I knew, was not imminent, I wanted to leave the diaries and journals I've been keeping since I was eleven years old to my granddaughter, Chloe . . . My daughter didn't even pause to consider the idea.

—Opening, *Things I Should Have Told My Daughter*, 2014

Pearl Cleage—playwright, journalist, novelist, poet, activist—was an active and enthusiastic participant in the movements that defined an era of great social change and upheaval throughout America. She calls herself "a sixties child," without irony or regret. With her writing and with her activism and with her clear, strong voice on the stage, in newspapers and magazines, in books, and in the classroom, she's been a player in one of our nation's most profound game changes, all the while making game-changing art.

Born to a schoolteacher and a minister, both civil rights activists, Pearl grew up in Detroit. Her father ran for governor of Michigan on the Freedom Now Party ticket. Following a stint at Howard University, Pearl transferred to Spelman College in Atlanta, where many of her books, and much of her life, would be set. Becoming active in local politics, she worked with Maynard Jackson, Atlanta's first African American mayor, before leaving city hall determined to become a full-time writer.

Her first memoir, *Things I Should Have Told My Daughter: Lies, Lessons & Love Affairs*, documents her growing awareness of feminism and of the role her writing would play in shaping her personal and professional lives. Her play *Flyin' West* was the most produced new play in the country in 1995, and her first novel, *What Looks Like Crazy on an Ordinary Day*, was a 1998 Oprah's Book Club pick and a *New York Times* bestseller.

"The purpose of my writing," Pearl Cleage has said, "is to explore the point where racism and sexism meet in me and are confronted by the power of truth and a genuine desire to live free." The power of her writing is clearly fueled by having adopted the same purpose for her well-lived life.

THE VITALS

Birthday: December 7, 1948

Born and raised: Detroit, Michigan

Home now: Atlanta, Georgia

Family: Married to Zaron Burnett, Jr.; daughter, Deignan Tucker; five grandchildren

Schooling: Howard University; bachelor's degree in drama, Spelman College

Day job: Mellon Playwright in Residence, Alliance Theatre, Atlanta, Georgia

Notable notes:

- Pearl won an NAACP Image Award in 2007 for her novel *Baby Brother's Blues*, the 2013 Theatre Legend Award from the Atlanta Black Theatre Festival, the 2010 Sankofa Freedom Award, and five AUDELCO Awards for Outstanding Achievement Off-Broadway for *Hospice*.
- Pearl's first novel was an Oprah's Book Club selection and spent nine weeks on the *New York Times* bestseller list.
- The author of more than a dozen plays, Pearl never thought she'd write a novel until she came up with a story that wouldn't fit into the structure of a play.

Facebook: https://www.facebook.com/pages/Pearl-Cleage/103365652761

Twitter: @pcleage

Website: www.pearlcleage.net

THE COLLECTED WORKS

Novels and Short Fiction

The Brass Bed and Other Stories, 1991

What Looks Like Crazy on an Ordinary Day, 1997

I Wish I Had a Red Dress, 2001

Some Things I Never Thought I'd Do, 2003

Babylon Sisters, 2005

Baby Brother's Blues, 2006

Seen It All and Done the Rest, 2008

Till You Hear From Me, 2010

Just Wanna Testify, 2011

Memoirs and Essays

Mad at Miles: A Blackwoman's Guide to Truth, 1990

Deals with the Devil and Other Reasons to Riot, 1993

Things I Should Have Told My Daughter: Lies, Lessons & Love Affairs, 2014

Plays (Partial Listing)

Puppetplay, 1988

Hospice, 1990

Flyin' West, 1992

Chain, 1992

Late Bus to Mecca, 1992

Blues for an Alabama Sky, 1995

Bourbon at the Border, 1997

A Song for Coretta, 2007

The Nacirema Society Requests the Honor of Your Presence at a Celebration of Their First One Hundred Years, 2010

What I Learned in Paris, 2012

Poetry

We Don't Need No Music, 1971

We Speak Your Names: A Celebration (with Zaron W. Burnett, Jr.), 2005

Pearl Cleage

Why I write about myself

I think of memoir as a book that connects the narrative of your life to an arc. My first nonfiction book, *Deals with the Devil,* was a collection of short pieces. Each piece was me reacting to a different issue. Many of them started as performance pieces or columns for the newspaper, so they were less me trying to talk about me and more me talking about the issues that were passing in front of me.

I've been keeping journals since I was eleven years old. When my granddaughter, Chloe, was three, I told my daughter that I wanted to give Chloe my journals when she turned sixteen. I thought it would be a wonderful gift to my granddaughter—so she could see a female life in progress, have a record of her grandmother's feminist journey. My daughter was completely unimpressed with that idea. She said, "Absolutely not. Those journals were written by you, meant for your eyes only. Your granddaughter doesn't need to know all of that."

I started thinking about her point of view and wondered if she was right. I wondered if the journals were valuable only to me. But when I reread them, I felt that they were valuable not only as a purely personal document of one life but as evidence that, as Anaïs Nin said, one life, deeply examined, ripples out to touch all other lives.

My own story includes my involvement in a number of social movements that were significant to the country. These included the civil rights movement, the Black Power movement, the antiwar movement, and the women's movement. I felt the journals were valuable because they were uncensored, deeply personal documentation of a specific life being lived, but also as a record of the impact of these social movements on one woman's life. For those reasons, I decided they were worth publishing.

Memoir merges the personal and the political

A lot of my fiction writing has been framed by the desire to place a personal story, preferably a love story, in the midst of someone's struggle for social change. In almost all my novels, there are women trying to make their neighborhoods better, for example by organizing their neighbors for civic action. Then they fall madly in love in the midst of fighting to make their neighborhood a better place.

For me, writing memoir is an effort to examine that place where the personal and the political become one; where you understand something because it's personal to you but you also then begin to understand the politics that connect your struggle to the struggles of other people. You recognize yourself as part of a whole.

I come to the political through an emotional, as well as intellectual, understanding of an issue. My novels *and* my nonfiction are grounded in the desire to make a reader *feel* something as well as *understand* something. People often want to make a distinction between literature that's grounded in an awareness of the individual within community and work that doesn't seem to be that, but everything takes place in some particular place, in some particular circumstance, and there are always politics that impact those particulars.

Sometimes there's a judgment made when politics are acknowledged and explored in fiction. These books may be labeled as something other than literature. Something less complex and less worthy of artistic attention. It's the same way a distinction is sometimes made between books written by women, where women are at the center of the story, and books written by men, with main characters who are male. When people use the term "chick lit" I find the term incredibly sexist. What would be the equivalent term that we'd apply to books where men are at the center of the story—*dick lit*?

You can't start breaking books off that way. The question is, is it a good story? Do we believe these characters? Do we care about what happens to them on their journeys?

The story dictates the genre

When I think of a story I want to tell, I know immediately whether it will be a novel or a memoir or a play. If it's a play, you can have only a certain number of characters, a certain number of settings, a certain length of time in which to tell that story. People will not sit in a theater for six or seven hours no matter how good the play is!

Sometimes there's a story that requires a great many characters, a lot more time, a larger number of settings in which to tell it. That could be a novel or a memoir. Before I start writing, I make sure I know what form I'm going to use and then I stick with that decision. Making that first choice to determine genre shapes all the other creative choices to come.

Having no secrets is a definite plus

I never worry about offending anybody when I'm writing fiction or plays. I don't write about real people, thinly disguised, and try to pretend they are fictional. My characters all begin in my imagination. It's easier to keep your family and friends that way!

When I'm writing about myself, I don't worry about keeping secrets. The fact is, I'm at a point in my life where I don't really have any secrets anymore. I have no fear that people will find out about something I did and think less of me. I have nothing to protect, which I think is crucial if you're going to write autobiographically. If you're going to write a memoir, you have to tell the truth as you know and remember it. Once you start smoothing your own rough edges, you might as well make it a novel.

The thing that was hardest to figure out was how to handle the affairs I had with men who were married. Some of these relationships played important roles in my life, but those were also the only times in my life when I felt I was really not living up to my own understanding of what was honorable behavior. I wasn't married at the time, but the men were. Having an affair is always wrong because you are agreeing to lie to cover up your own bad behavior. Talking about those relationships didn't make me look so good, but I wanted to show my own growth and development as a free woman who consciously committed to telling the truth about all things. No exceptions! It wasn't fun to admit the times I strayed from that commitment, but I had to do it.

Yes, there was a moment when I thought, Should I really write about this? But the answer was yes. It was part of the book's narrative. I was part of the generation that grew up with the birth control pill. Many of us questioned what was then conventional morality. Some of us didn't believe in monogamy and traditional marriage, which was fine, but that didn't excuse us from trying to behave as honorable women within those changing definitions. It was still necessary to commit to the truth. Just think what would happen if women all stood up one day and said they'd never lie to one another again. The power of truth and sisterhood that would be unleashed would be amazing!

Protect the innocent

What did worry me when I was writing my memoir was the people who would appear in my stories simply because they happened to pass through my life. I'm very conscious of not telling other people's secrets, or revealing things about people that would make them uncomfortable or unhappy in any way, because that's not fair.

I respect the privacy of real people. Sometimes I change

04/03/2018

Item(s) Checked Out

TITLE   Why we write about
BARCODE   33029100732205
DUE DATE   **04-24-18**

Thank you for visiting the library!

Sacramento Public Library

www.saclibrary.org

names and details so the person being written about knows it's him or her but no one else does. I asked only three people for permission to use their real names—my daughter, my ex-husband, and a very close friend who married a high-level government official—and they all said yes. They trusted me to get it right, to tell the story straight. I found that most people actually enjoyed being included.

I love my friends. I love my family. And I have a wealth of material without having to betray anyone. I don't have an ax to grind with anyone I've written about. I know people sometimes use memoirs to settle old scores, to get their version of the story on record, but I'm not one of them.

Memoir means getting messy

I wanted to speak as a woman of my age to younger women, who sometimes will encounter me now, when so many areas of my life look calm and serene, and assume that I was this way when I was twenty-five or thirty-two or forty-two.

I know some women my own age who will encourage younger women in the belief that we were never as messy as they are. That we were so much smarter than they will ever be. What's the point? If they can see growth in us and in the flow of our lives, they certainly will be more patient with their own journeys. I love Anaïs Nin's diaries. I remember being really moved by the way she talked so openly about the contradictions in her life; about the times she didn't live up to her own high ideals. It was great to read such a truthful account of a real woman's life. I hope my books can do that for young women. I hope they can find value in my struggles to lead an honest, interesting life.

Of course life is messy, but you have to keep trying to move ahead. You have to keep telling the truth with all the messiness in it. In that, I think I'm a great example. I'm not perfect, but I'm free, I'm happy, I'm a good person. So I get to say, "Live your messy life! Be bold! Be strong! Be truthful and don't bore yourself to death."

Push toward the truth

When I wrote the memoir, my goal was to push myself to tell the truth. To tell a story that was interesting. To turn myself into a character people would want to spend three hundred pages with. To invite people into the flow of a life in progress.

This required really looking at myself. I had to decide if I was interesting enough to tell these stories of my own life. I had to find those moments that would make a narrative arc, that would allow me to weave a coherent story from the various elements of my real life.

I wanted to show how my life intersected with the civil rights and feminist movements. *Things I Should Have Told My Daughter* isn't just my personal story. It's a story of people who were trying to change the country. Some of the people I wrote about have recognizable names, but to me, they were friends and comrades.

Don't write a memoir to prove you're right

When my daughter told me that I should burn my journals and be done with it, I was really surprised and a little hurt. I love my journals! Initially I was moved to write a memoir by the impetus to prove her wrong and prove myself right.

Once I started reading through the journals systematically, the thing that moved me was my real desire, throughout my lifetime, to tell the truth. I could see myself trying to figure out what the right thing was and how to do it, even if I was scared. I felt protective of myself for doing things that weren't always the safest or smartest things to do, but I risked it because I was trying to get to the emotional truth of whatever moment I was in. I wanted to be an artist and to grow into an honorable person and a free woman.

What surprised me most were the letters from my mother, which I hadn't read in a long, long time. I hesitated about putting them in the book. But they were such an important part of my life at that time—my concern over my mother being ill, knowing that she was not going to get any better. I loved our growing understanding of each other through the letters we were writing back and forth with increasing urgency. I felt like I got to know my mother as a woman, in the months before she died, in a way I never had before; and I will always be grateful for that. My mother's passing was so important to my own realization that I was a grown woman. I understood then that there was nobody to stand between me and the shaping and living of my own life.

Activism is fuel

I was raised in a movement household. Everything we did was grounded in being part of the African American freedom struggle. Later, when I was married and about to become a mother, I discovered feminism and participated actively in the women's movement.

I never experienced my activism as a burden. It was a wonderful source of energy and a wonderful source of material for my writing. I didn't find it grim. Some of the most romantic love stories take place in the midst of the most serious historical moments. Look at *Casablanca*. It's exhilarating to fight for freedom and fall madly in love at the same time! That's what often happens to the characters in my books. The reason they're fighting in the first place is so they can move around and live as the free people they are. They're freedom fighters, but they're already living free, just like I was.

I was fully involved in trying to end racial segregation and gender oppression. And I was also having great times, passionate affairs, drinking champagne, smoking marijuana, dancing in the aisles at a Rolling Stones concert. It was all a great adventure.

This is what sixty-five looks like

At the heart of it for me is having a big, full, meaningful life that doesn't end when you hit your sixties. I have a good friend I've known since we were in our twenties. We went out for drinks when she turned forty and talked about how people stop having adventures when they start getting older. So we took an oath and swore that we would never stop having our adventures. So far, so good.

I remember seeing that old Gloria Steinem comment on a T-shirt, "This is what forty looks like." Now I need one that reads: "This is what sixty-five looks like." It's very different from what I thought this moment would be. I've done so many things that my mother and my grandmothers could hardly imagine. Neither of my grandmothers could drive a car, and they lived in Detroit! Neither one ever worked outside her house once she got married. I have a very different life than they had, but I always feel the pleasure of building on the things they taught me. They'd love to know what I'm doing now and I think they'd approve of my grandmothering skills.

Pearl Cleage's Wisdom for Memoir Writers

- Ask yourself the question, Am I prepared to tell the truth, the whole truth, and nothing but the truth? If you say yes, you have an opportunity to write something wonderful. If there are lots of things that are off limits, try writing fiction instead.

- Ask yourself if you're prepared to make yourself vulnerable and not care about people's judgments. If you're not yet who you want to be, keep working on your life and write about it later.

- Before you subject the other people in your life to the scrutiny that comes with having your story, and theirs, in print, ask them for their permission. If people have strong objections, you should seriously consider honoring their requests.

- Don't burn your journals. You might want those written recollections years from now when you're ready to write your memoir.

CHAPTER FOUR

Pat Conroy

I've been writing the story of my own life for over forty years. My own stormy autobiography has been my theme, my dilemma, my obsession, and the fly-by-night dread I bring to the art of fiction.

—Opening, *The Death of Santini*, 2013

Some novelists are dragged out from behind the fictional veil and into the spotlight of memoir, in various states of unwillingness, propelled by life-changing events that would otherwise gnaw holes in their minds. They write the memoir, tell the story, go back to novel writing.

Other memoirists commit to the form early and often, tackling a hot topic or two from one angle and then another.

And still others alternate between fiction and non-, depending on the material and the mood.

Not Pat Conroy. Nearly everything he writes, he says, is autobiographical; each book is an attempt to heal from the abusive childhood that shaped but has not defined him.

Thirty-five years before he finally wrote about his abusive father in explicit form, Pat Conroy fictionalized the same material in his 1976 novel, *The Great Santini*—a book that couldn't have caused more discord in his family if it had been labeled "memoir." His marriage ended. Relatives picketed his book events, telling fans not to buy the book. Eventually, in a plot twist worthy of the finest fiction, the novel helped reconcile Pat and his father. "I hope you enjoy my son's latest work of fiction," the elder Conroy would write when asked to sign copies of his son's book.

But writing a slew of autobiographical novels wasn't enough to cure what ailed Pat Conroy. "This year I turned sixty-five," he writes in *The Death of Santini*. "I've come to realize that I still carry the bruised freight of that childhood every day . . . It weighs me down and fills me with dread . . . I've got to try to make sense of it one last time, a final circling of the block, a reckoning."

THE VITALS

Birthday: October 26, 1945

Born and raised: Atlanta, Georgia

Home now: Beaufort, South Carolina

Family: Married to Cassandra King; four children

Schooling: The Citadel

Day job: Nope

Notable notes:
- Describing his origins, Pat says he was "the first of seven children of a career military officer and a Southern beauty."
- Pat was fired from his teaching job in a one-room schoolhouse in South Carolina because he refused to allow corporal punishment of his students. He wrote about this experience in his 1972 book *The Water Is Wide*.

- Pat's 1986 novel *The Prince of Tides* sold more than five million copies and was made into an Oscar-nominated film starring Barbra Streisand and Nick Nolte.

Facebook: https://www.facebook.com/PatConroyAuthor

Website: www.patconroy.com

THE COLLECTED WORKS

Memoirs

My Losing Season, 2002

My Reading Life, 2010

The Death of Santini, 2013

Novels

The Boo, 1969

The Water Is Wide, 1972

The Great Santini, 1976

The Lords of Discipline, 1980

The Prince of Tides, 1986

Beach Music, 1995

South of Broad, 2009

Cookbook

The Pat Conroy Cookbook, 2004

Film Adaptations

Conrack, 1974

The Great Santini, 1979

The Prince of Tides, 1991

Pat Conroy

Why I write about myself

In 2002 I published my first memoir, *My Losing Season*, about my year as captain of The Citadel basketball team. I wrote it because I wanted to tell the truth about the harsh culture of The

Citadel and my relationship with the coach. That led to writing about the harsh reality of my family.

I waited more than a decade to start writing my second memoir. I'd always wanted to tell the full story of my family, but I had to wait until my parents died. I wanted my readers to know where all my fiction came from. I wanted my memoir to be based not only on what I'd experienced but also on what my brothers and sisters thought of it all. And I knew I wanted to wait to write it until we had time to age into it—to let it ripen somewhat and to look back on what had happened.

When I was researching *The Death of Santini*, I found out some things that absolutely staggered me. My brothers and sisters remembered almost nothing. Each of them remembered only certain things. Much of what they remembered were things I'd written about fictionally. So my "fiction" became part of the memoir.

The same thing happened when I was writing about The Citadel. I went back to get the memories of my classmates about the plebe system and our horrible first year. Most of the guys who survived had simply repressed what happened.

I began to think that some of us are the designated rememberers. Why do we remember? I don't know. But I think that's why memoir interests us—because we're the ones who pass the stories.

Fiction: stranger than truth

Fiction contains memoir; memoir contains fiction.

Funny things happen when you're writing fiction. Because my father died at the end of my novel *The Great Santini*, when I introduced people to my father in real life, they'd say to him, "Wait! I read about your funeral."

Storytelling is so much more powerful than I'd ever realized. People will take whatever story you tell to be the literal truth. I've had guys I've never seen before come up to me at book readings and say they were my college roommates. I used to think they were just crazies. Now I think it's an imaginative jump they've made, a spark across the night. They somehow actually believe that.

I wrote about a basketball game that took place in 1967. I must have had five thousand people tell me they were there that night. The stadium holds only five thousand! Did I run into every one of them?

I taught in a high school for two years after I was at The Citadel. My brothers and sisters said they've met endless numbers of people who said they were in my classes during that time.

My fiction has become so interwoven with my nonfiction that it has confused everybody, including my brothers and sisters, even though I interviewed them about it before I wrote it. Except for my poet sister Carol, who has disappeared from my life, my siblings and I have been doing panels together about *The Death of Santini*. It's been fascinating to hear their insights.

My brother Jim surprised me during the latest panel we were on. He said, "I can tell the difference between fiction and nonfiction. My father was a total asshole and Pat has always painted him as much too nice. That's fiction!"

All's fair in love and memoir

My teammates at The Citadel were all concerned when they heard I was working on *My Losing Season*. Most of them had never had a book in their homes. They'd never read another book in their lives. They said, "We don't want you to do a book. You don't make an honest living. All you do is you make shit up about us." Their wives were terrified. Their children were terrified. Everyone was scared to death I'd be making up stuff about them.

I said, "Guys, relax. Here's what you don't know. I'll go over every little thing with y'all. We're going to talk about conversations we had thirty years ago. None of them will be true word for word. What we'll aim for is the spirit of those conversations, the flavor of those conversations."

I ended up calling all these guys a million times. I'd call Zipper and I'd tell him, "Rube said this; Zipper, do you remember that conversation?" Then Zipper would say, "Rube's fulla shit." I kept going from one guy to the next. Some guys remembered almost nothing. Some trusted my version of the entire experience. Some guys had amazing memories. I wanted all of them. I told the guys I interviewed, "When the book comes out, and you read it, you need to remember that it's some version of the truth, even though I'm telling you right now it's probably not going to be yours."

The guy I worried about most was the one who suffered the most the year I wrote about in the book. He said, "Conroy, I don't trust you. I read your other books. Look what you did to your old man! To your son! If that's what you did to your family in your other books, I can tell you I'm going to hate this one."

After the book came out, that guy stood up and said, "No one is more knowledgeable than I am, and every word in that book was true." As a professional writer I know that that's an impossibility. But it was good to hear.

Truth and loss

My sister Carol isn't speaking to me. She wouldn't speak to me at our mother's funeral. She said we had a toxic family. I said, "No shit. I've been making a living off that toxic family my whole life."

Since *The Death of Santini* came out, none of us has heard a word from her. I'm sure she's furious about her portrait in the book.

Of course I've wondered why Carol isn't speaking to me. She might be mad at me for talking about her coming out as a lesbian. She could be mad that I mentioned her first girlfriend's name. She's a poet, and she's very private. Her privacy means everything to her. She's fiercely guarded. You will not find her giving interviews to anybody about anything.

The only time she's broken that rule was for an odd CNN Conroy Thanksgiving special when Dad was still alive. He had cancer. It was his last year alive. We all got together, and Carol finally accepted me and Dad and the family for what we were.

The reunion was phony. Everyone knew it. It was the most uncomfortable scene since the Pilgrims sat down with the Native Americans after Plymouth Rock. I watched the show and I thought, My God in heaven, what a travesty of a festive moment. It was so painful.

When you write memoir, who are you hurting? It's always

been the great taboo: hurting your parents, hurting your family, hurting your children—although I tell my children I can't wait to write about their hellion teenage years, when they dated the most hideous boys in America just to torture me.

If I'm writing a portrait of my family and I don't talk about the effect of that family on Carol, my beloved sister, if I don't talk about how her childhood ruined her life, I'd be a liar and an unfit witness for the family I've been writing about. I decided that if I'm going to write about this, I want to write the truth as I know it, as I lived it.

When it comes to memoir, I'll always choose the writer over the person who suffers because of what's written.

Truth: relative

People who read my memoirs ask me how I know what's true and what's not true. I don't worry about it too much. I understand memoir and fiction, and I understand that there's making up going on with both.

I've seen memoirists who go nuts for absolute scrupulous word-for-word truth telling. It's an impossible standard. If you have to write it perfectly, the story won't be told. Here's what I know: If a story is not told, it's the silence around that untold story that ends up killing people. The story can open up a secret to the light.

When you write a memoir, you want it to be as true as you can make it. With fiction you have a much larger body of water to play in. But I have to admit this right away: I'm swimming in dangerous water when I talk about the difference between memoir and fiction. I've often intermingled the two.

Trying to figure out where the truth lies is one of the perils of writing memoir.

Truth: hard to believe

I had trouble with *The Great Santini* because my very proper editor said, in her British accent, "Pat, it's simply not believable that a father would treat a son in this extraordinary way." I had to clean up the book to make it believable to people who went to Harvard.

I was easy on my father in that book. I wasn't yet prepared to say he beat us half to death and left us in the driveway. I had trouble getting people to believe me. There was an article in *The Atlantic* magazine saying that I'd made the whole thing up. My father told them, "If anything, I was too good a father. My son has a vivid imagination."

I wrote a letter to the editor, saying, Yeah, I made the whole thing up. My father was a Carmelite nun. I used my imagination to make everything up.

Memoir matters

Memoir has been necessary for my life. I've found writers whose voices I can trust. In their memoirs they came out and told me things I needed to know about how to live a life. If not for those writers telling me how to look for truth in life, how to know it's there when you find it, I don't know who I'd be.

Memoir is a deal with the devil

I'm glad I made it out of that last memoir alive, except for Carol. I can't tell you how much I regret losing my sister, and I can't say she's wrong to have those feelings. I suffered over that. I suffer still. When you write memoir, that's part of the bargain you make with God and the devil.

Pat Conroy's Wisdom for Memoir Writers

- A memoir is not a newspaper article. It's not expected to be word-for-word true. If you have to write it perfectly, the story won't be told, and the most important thing is that you tell your story.
- Don't hang around with writers. We're all crazy and we won't do your writing any good.
- Memoirs hurt people. Secrets hurt people. The question to ask yourself is, if you tell your story, will it do enough good to make it worth hurting people?

CHAPTER FIVE

Kelly Corrigan

When I was growing up, my mom was guided by the strong belief that to befriend me was to deny me the one thing I really needed to survive childhood: a mother. Consequently, we were never one of those Mommy & Me pairs who sat close or giggled.

—Opening, *Glitter and Glue*, 2014

Oakland, California, author, photographer, fund-raiser, mom, community servant, and all-around good person Kelly Corrigan is forty-seven years old, with few extraordinary events in her life to report—and three blockbuster, bestselling memoirs to her name.

How, one might ask (and many have), could one so young and well-adjusted fill the pages of *three* memoirs? Does our seemingly insatiable hunger to know the intimate details of other people's lives explain the success of this well-educated, well-loved, middle-class white woman, whose writings reveal an all-too-common bout with breast cancer and an all-too-rare bond with her adored dad (*The Middle Place*), a passionate yet predominant set of maternal intentions (*Lift*), and a midlife reconciliation with her mother, who told her, "Your father's the glitter but I'm the glue" (*Glitter and Glue*)?

Kelly Corrigan's literary celebrity rests on that very ordinariness, known in publishing circles as "relatability." It all started in 2008, when Kelly wrote and then read a five-minute ode to women's friendships to a group of women sitting in someone's living room. The talk was recorded and posted on YouTube, and "Transcending" became the proverbial Internet sensation, with close to five million views.

At a moment when the publishing industry was frantically producing more and more sophisticated book trailers in hopes that these mini movies would revive the industry's sinking sales, "Transcending" turned Kelly's first memoir, *The Middle Place*, into a runaway bestseller.

In life and in literature, Kelly deserves the acclaim. Having survived breast cancer, she founded the patient-support website Circus of Cancer. Grateful for her daughter's successful treatment for meningitis at Children's Hospital Oakland, she created Notes & Words, an annual fund-raiser at Oakland's Paramount Theatre that has raised more than $4 million for the hospital in its first five years.

"People are struggling; make yourself useful," Kelly advises readers on her website. This is her ordinary brilliance: an irresistible cocktail of lyrical writing and solid, useful insight; the everyday magic that makes her legions of devoted readers hope that her third memoir won't be her last.

THE VITALS

Birthday: August 16, 1967

Born and raised: Radnor, Pennsylvania

Home now: Piedmont, California

Family: Married to Edward Lichty since 2000; two children, Georgia (b. 2001) and Claire (b. 2003)

Schooling: Radnor High School; University of Richmond; master's in literature, San Francisco State University

Day job: Director and host of *Foreword*, digital conversation series on Medium.com

Notable notes:
- Kelly's first memoir, a look at identity called *The Middle Place*, was inspired by her late-stage breast cancer diagnosis at thirty-six, which was followed three months later by her adored dad's bladder cancer diagnosis.
- Kelly is currently writing her first novel.
- Now in its sixth year, the Notes & Words fund-raiser Kelly founded has raised more than $4 million.

Facebook: https://www.facebook.com/kellycorriganauthor?ref =hl

Twitter: @corrigankelly

Website: www.kellycorrigan.com

THE COLLECTED WORKS

Memoirs

The Middle Place, 2008

Lift, 2010

Glitter and Glue, 2014

Essays, Features (Partial Listing)

Medium.com

O, The Oprah Magazine

Good Housekeeping

Glamour

Kelly Corrigan

Why I write about myself

I didn't stand back and survey the landscape of literary forms and choose memoir. I wrote *The Middle Place* because I was told my dad was dying and I wanted to put on paper what it had been like to be his daughter. I had this very clear vision of handing my dad a manuscript (I even imagined how I would get it bound; this was just at the dawn of self-publishing) and saying, "You are the cornerstone of everything. Being your kid is the luckiest thing that ever happened to me." I wrote all the stories from growing up, the ones I knew by heart, the ones I had told a thousand times. I found a self-publishing site that I could afford, and my graphic artist friend, Rocky Laber, figured out how to lay it out and paginate it so it looked like a real book and we sent it off to some printing house in Indiana. About three weeks later, I got a dozen copies in the mail, and about a week after that, I handed a copy to my dad in the kitchen of my childhood home.

Then my sister-in-law got ahold of the pages, and she gave

them to her buddy Jack Horner, who had just left a literary agency called ICM. He sent it over to a woman who was kind of new there, Andy Barzvi, who I learned later had just lost her dad to cancer. Andy became my agent, and she sold the book in three days.

Once I got the hang of writing, I felt that I had a few other things I'd like to put on paper. As a lifelong journal keeper, processing my life on the page was second nature. And once I went on book tour and experienced the outrageous joy of reading to an audience of readers, which is about the most fun I can have legally, I knew I would do it again. Assuming they would let me.

Self-flagellation can be very motivating

There are seven billion people on the planet. I think something like one million books come out every year in the United States. Go to a bookstore. Take in the sheer volume. When I start to get self-conscious or panicky, I like to call up my mother, who will set me right with her favorite line: Oh, for God's sake, Kelly, who's looking at you?

That said, when I cave to worry, which of course I do, I think about all the smart, talented writers out there and how they must think I'm very lucky to have ever been published. And of course, they would be right.

When I really want to torture myself, I picture all the great brains I know, friends of my husband's from Yale or Stanford, talking about what a sweet foolish girl I am, out there calling myself "a writer," with a mix of pity and tenderness in their voices.

On the best of days, all this self-flagellation makes me work harder to wrestle with every sentence, to not give up on a piece too soon. I think a lot about Mary Karr and Calvin Trillin and Frank McCourt and how deft they have been with the form. So careful. Controlled. Masterful. They don't leave a page before it is ready. Their work is never undercooked. That's hard. That's tiring. That takes a poet's focus and patience. I'm working on that. I tell myself all the time: "Write like this is the last thing you're ever going to get to say."

There are limits to what I'll disclose (about other people)

I don't mind talking about myself, especially my past self. I haven't talked nearly as much about my marriage or sex or money. So clearly, I have a ways to go before I can say I am truly an open book.

With my husband, though I do intend to write our story down at some point, I do worry that a book about us might jinx what we have. It's a nice, easy relationship, for the most part, and I fear that if I wrote about it too much, that would mean that I had thought about it and talked about it too much, which could somehow infect the marriage with a consciousness that wouldn't serve it. That marriage of mine is the center of everything. It must be tended above all. But then I read Ann Patchett's memoir about her second marriage and thought, It's doable; there's a way.

I can no longer tell stories involving my daughters. They are tweens; they have no sense of humor about themselves anymore. That's probably the number one reason I'm moving to fiction for the next book.

I don't write books to impress my mother—but it doesn't hurt

My mother's a big reader and not too quick with the compliments. When my first book was bought by a publisher, she said, "Who's gonna want to read about us? We're not rich, we're not poor. We're not smart, we're not dumb. We're totally average."

I shrugged and said, "I don't know, Ma, but the publisher thinks it will work out. So I guess we leave that to them."

Then, as soon as *The Middle Place* came out, my mother started dropping by the bookstore near her office once or twice a week (seriously—that frequently) and moving the books. She didn't like where they shelved *The Middle Place*, so she'd take all the copies down and put them near the cash registers or the *People* magazine rack or right on top of the big bestsellers at the time, like Suze Orman's book.

I always imagined Mrs. Orman, Suze's mom, coming through the store after my mom had been there, and complaining to management that some no-name had stuck a piece of crap on top of her daughter's latest blockbuster.

Memoir is not without controversy

I don't want to fan the flame on this, but one of my brothers didn't really get what I was doing at first. He thought with *The Middle Place* that I was exposing our family in a way that could be damaging or hurtful.

The thing of it was, I don't think he understood the form. He had probably never read a memoir, or if he had, it was Wayne Gretzky's or Lee Iaccoca's, which are more like autobiographies. So he was anxious about how the publication would pan out.

He feels good now. On this last tour, for *Glitter and Glue*, he came to every New York reading—three in a row. I was obsessed with his reaction to my talk. I so wanted his blessing. Finally, one night over a pitcher of beer, he said that I "blew him away." I waited forty years for his approval. For a little sister, that's pretty much nirvana.

It's pretty simple, really: I write for my readers

The reaction of my readers has a huge influence on me—probably more than is healthy or helpful.

At this point, after hundreds of readings over seven years, I know exactly what people like about my books; what type of stories they respond to. I can hear them laugh when I write something I know they'll totally get, something that will make them say, "Exactly!"

I'm worried that they'll all leave me the minute I switch to fiction. Sometimes, at readings, there's so much affection. They touch me on the arm when I'm signing. Sometimes they ask for a hug, and I think, If I hand you a novel, you're going to say, "No, no, no! I don't want your imagination! I want you, I want the real stuff, I want to hear what you did when you found out your kids were having sex or smoking weed or stealing bathing suits from H&M . . . I want to compare notes!"

But there are actually things I want to talk about that I cannot in a memoir. I'm not going to detail the worst arguments I've ever had with my husband, the secret insecurities my daughters have trusted me with over the years, the excruciating story of my father-in-law's childhood. I'm definitely not in the Anything for Art camp. I am a person first, writer second. I will not violate my relationships. But in a novel, I can go anywhere. I can show the nastiest, most pitiful, regrettable sides of myself and everyone I know. I can expose every nerve. Consequently, I find it's turning out to be much easier to write without the (understandable) boundaries memoir imposes.

Writing is solitary confinement

Even though I seem to get a lot done, between Notes & Words, *Foreword* on Medium.com, and the books, I'm often quite lonely and kind of lost, totally unsure of my next move. I really struggle with the solitary confinement writing requires.

I am a class A extrovert; I'm completely enlivened by the presence of others. The adrenaline transforms me. I can have a fever of 102 the day of a reading and I'll bang back some Tylenol, crawl out of bed, and lug myself across town, thinking, I can't do this tonight. But once I see all those readers crowded in the bookstore, my book in their laps, it's game on. (Though, on the way home, I almost always fold my jacket into a pillow and go fetal in the back of the car.) Monday mornings, I can't bring myself to put on a bra and get out of the house; I wander around my kitchen cleaning the dust that settles into the tiny ledges of our Shaker cabinets, muttering to the dog about what I should be doing. That's not at all how I feel in a social setting and it's probably not how I come off on the page either.

My readers might also be surprised to know that I am often totally unmotivated and fail to complete even the simplest assignments I give myself. Like I'll I tell myself, "Write nonstop for x minutes. No getting up for tea, no checking e-mail, no answering the phone." And sometimes, even when I'm only shooting for twenty minutes, I fail. It's so pathetic. But then somehow these books get written. I can't even really figure out how that happens. I think I black out.

Do unto others

I don't reveal much about others in my memoirs. I think of myself as an entertainer—not a moral leader, not a judge or a jury.

I have been surprised, during the drafting of each manuscript, what my family does and does not object to. Like my mother, with the first book, *The Middle Place*; after she read it top to bottom, she called and said, "Kelly, it's beautiful. However . . ." And I was so sure she was going to tell me to take out the story about losing my virginity or the chapter about how my mother "regifts" just about anything people give her (unless it's monogrammed). But those things weren't the problem at all. In fact, she said, "Oh, for God's sake, Kelly, that's not it. First of all, you were probably the last virgin on the Eastern Seaboard, and second of all, Betty Moran told me regifting is green. I don't think you should tell the whole world that you got drunk as a sophomore in high school."

I tried to convince her that most people I know got drunk as sophomores in high school, but she kept bugging me to take it out. Finally I said, "Ma, I would change it if the story were about you, but—" And she interrupted me to say, "That story *is* about me. That was on my watch!"

Kelly Corrigan's Wisdom for Memoir Writers

- *Write every day.* Even if all you do is tweak a few lines, change the fonts, move the margins—anything to put you in the chair, in the headspace, in the zone. There's tremendous value in keeping the story and the themes in your subconscious mind.

- Post your work where people can find it. I use Medium.com, which has something like twenty million readers a month, and I find that I work harder when I know the work might be read by people I don't know.

- Be careful who you show your early work to. Good lay editors are hard to find. You need someone who can think at the highest level about the fundamental drivers of good narrative: characters, scene, tension, arc, pacing . . . And while we're talking about feedback, be careful not to collect too much. In the end, this is your work alone. Writing is not a team sport.

- Trust yourself. If you've remembered something very well—a fight, a kiss, a plane ride, a certain stranger— there's a reason. Keep writing until you figure out the significance of your most vivid memories.

CHAPTER SIX

Edwidge Danticat

*The morning Claire Limyè Lanmè Faustin turned seven, a
freak wave, measuring between ten and twelve feet high,
was seen in the ocean outside of Ville Rose. Claire's father,
Nozias, a fisherman, was one of many who saw it in the
distance as he walked toward his sloop.*

—Opening, *Claire of the Sea Light*, 2013

At age twelve, Haitian-born Edwidge Danticat spoke Haitian Creole and French, not English. At age twenty-six,
she was a graduate of Barnard College with a published novel
(in English) and an MFA in creative writing from Brown
University—and the youngest nominee ever for the National
Book Award. Oprah chose Edwidge's first novel, *Breath, Eyes,
Memory*, for her book club selection in 1998, when Edwidge
was a ripe old twenty-nine.

Since then, Edwidge Danticat has continued to rack up literary nominations, prizes, and awards the way most writers accumulate rejection letters. She was named one of "20 people in
their twenties who will make a difference" by *Harper's Bazaar*,
one of "30 Artists Under 30 Most Likely to Change the Culture in the Next 30 Years" by *The New York Times Magazine*,

and one of the "15 Gutsiest Women of the Year" by *Jane* magazine. *Granta* magazine anointed her one of "20 Best Young American Novelists" in 1996; *The New Yorker* included her on its list of twenty exemplars of "American fiction of the future" in 1999. In 2009, she received a MacArthur Foundation Fellowship.

None of this acclaim results from playing it safe. Edwidge Danticat writes, speaks, and demonstrates her beliefs, particularly where justice for the Haitian people is concerned. Fellow Caribbean writer Robert Antoni said that she is "doing for Haiti's history of violence and vengeance what Toni Morrison did for the U.S. in tackling the horrors of slavery and its aftermath."

As she lives, so she writes, experimenting with each new book. "Although everybody from Oprah to *The New Yorker* has tried to own her," writer Caryl Phillips wrote, "Edwidge ploughs an independent furrow, and her work gets stronger and more confident with each book."

Edwidge's portfolio is even more exceptional in light of her origins. Born in Port-au-Prince during the dictatorial Duvalier regime, she and her younger brother were placed in her uncle's home—"a house filled with children whose parents had migrated to other countries"—when her father, and then her mother, left to find work in New York. "At the airport my uncle had to peel me off my mother's body," Edwidge has said. "I retreated into silence."

Silence—and books. An avid reader, Edwidge became a writer when her father sent her a typewriter. And the rest is . . . her story.

THE VITALS

Birthday: January 19, 1969

Born and raised: Port-au-Prince, Haiti, and Brooklyn, New York

Home now: Miami, Florida

Family: Husband Fedo Boyer, daughters Mira and Leila

Schooling: Clara Barton High School, Barnard College, and Brown University; honorary doctor of letters from Brown University in 2008, Smith College in 2012, and Yale University in 2013

Day job: Teaching creative writing at the University of Miami

Notable notes:

- Edwidge starred in an indie film called *Stones in the Sun* and was an extra in the film adaptation of Toni Morrison's *Beloved*. She also worked with filmmakers Jonathan Demme and Patricia Benoit on documentaries about Haiti.
- When she enrolled at Barnard, Edwidge was planning to become a nurse. Instead, she graduated with a BA in French literature.

Facebook: https://www.facebook.com/edwidgedanticat

Website: www.edwidgedanticat.com

THE COLLECTED WORKS

Novels

Breath, Eyes, Memory, 1994

The Farming of Bones, 1998

The Dew Breaker, 2004

Claire of the Sea Light, 2013

Nonfiction

After the Dance, 2002

Create Dangerously, 2010

Anthologies

The Butterfly's Way, 2001

Haiti Noir, 2011

The Best American Essays, 2011

Haiti Noir 2, 2013

Children's Books

Eight Days, 2010

The Last Mapou, 2013

Untwine, 2015

Mama's Nightingale, 2015

Short Story Collection

Krik? Krak!, 1996

Memoir

Brother, I'm Dying, 2007

Young Adult Novels

Behind the Mountains, 2002

Anacaona, 2005

Edwidge Danticat

Why I write about myself

Each time I write memoir, in short or long form, something happens that compels me to do it—something that feels pressing and urgent, something that there is no other way to express.

I wrote my first published essay when I was fourteen years

old. I joined the student staff of a citywide high school newspaper called *New Youth Connections* and at the first meeting I was assigned to write about the way my family celebrates Christmas. I would have never imagined that people would be interested in something like how my family celebrates Christmas. I didn't think there was anything special about it even though we were Haitians and relatively new to the United States and had rituals that were just ours. My family was also Pentecostal, which added a certain religious fervor to our Christmas. I took all of that for granted because it was so familiar to me. I didn't think anyone would be interested in it.

When I write about myself I always imagine the person or persons I'm sharing with as people I am really close to: family, friends, and intimates. I think that is the only way I can convince myself that an eager audience is waiting to hear these very personal things from me.

In 2007, I published a memoir called *Brother, I'm Dying*. The book just walked up to me and knocked me over the head and demanded to be written. I wrote about a year, 2004, which was the two-hundred-year anniversary of Haitian independence. During that year, there was a coup in Haiti that unseated the same democratically elected president a second time.

That same year my father was diagnosed with end-state pulmonary fibrosis. My eighty-one-year-old uncle—the uncle who helped raised me in Haiti—died in immigration custody while requesting asylum in the United States. All this happened while I was pregnant with my first child, my daughter Mira. I didn't intend to write a memoir until maybe I was eighty years old. But writing about this whirlwind of events and emotions was the only way I could stay sane. It was such a terrible and beautiful year that I wanted to capture it somehow.

If I were a painter, I would have found some way to paint a series of paintings about that year. If I were a musician, I would have written a piece of music. If I were a dancer, I would have choreographed something. But since I'm a writer, this was the only place I could go to. So I wrote what I called not a memoir— a *me*-moir—but a *we*-moir, about my dad, my uncle, and my newborn daughter, among others.

In the book, I say, "I am writing this because they can't." "They" being my uncle and my father, who both died during that period of time. After the experience of writing that book and seeing how relatively well it was received, I realized that in writing the most singular things, we might be able to reach out and move others. So I write memoir because there are people in my family who no longer can. I write memoir to honor their lives and share their stories. George Meredith said, "Memoirs are the backstairs of history." I want to find those backstairs over and over and keep a map of them for future generations. I write memoir for the next generation of my family and others yet unborn. I also write memoir for the same reason I read memoirs; with the hope that my story might connect me with others. I write memoir to feel less alone.

It's easier to write about you than me

I float a lot between genres, so I don't see memoir as a permanent genre for me. Unless I have something really urgent to say, I can't imagine constantly writing 50,000 to 100,000 words about myself. I would worry about being like that person at a party who can't stop talking about himself or herself. I don't have that instant sense of perspective about events as they're happening to me. I really admire people who have it. I just don't have it. I need time. I need distance. So I've often masked memoir in a less personal frame.

For example, a couple of years ago I wrote a book about carnival in Haiti, a book called *After the Dance*. In that book, I was able to write about myself and my return trips to Haiti within this journalistic, travelogue frame of being an observer and later a participant at carnival. That way if the memoir part is boring, there's another layer for the reader to hold on to and remain engaged with.

I'd much rather write about others than about myself. But you have to let the material guide you. It's hard to explain this in a very replicable way. But I think instinctively you know what should be written in what way. I sometimes rewrite my essays as fiction so I can add material to them that didn't happen. I use scenes from my articles in my novels. I love using my nonfiction—memoir included—to make my fiction feel more "real."

Welcome to my bathroom. I'm naked

I think it's inevitable to feel exposed. I always feel a bit naked at first, as though I've just opened the door to my shower and let a bunch of people in there.

I feel exposed. I feel raw. I feel vulnerable. I always worry what people close to me are going to think or say. It feels to me as though there are people waiting around with knives, waiting to skewer me.

When it's fiction, it's easier to accept public criticism. But when it's memoir, they're not talking about just a book. They're also talking about your life. When *Brother, I'm Dying* came out, it was hard not to take the reviews personally in a way that I don't take reviews of my fiction personally. One reviewer said that I was cold. Another said that I was making myself sound like a dutiful daughter, like a good girl.

Some people who review memoirs don't discuss craft in the books at all. Many of them simply discuss your personality and the way you present yourself. So I'm always anticipating that.

I was trying to make something artful while writing my memoir, but I also felt as though each time I sat down to write, I was visiting with my dad and uncle after they died. Writing that book was therapeutic in a way that writing no other book has ever been for me. I felt shielded by that greater purpose to my story. I felt protected by the love I felt for my father and uncle and for my newborn daughter. I would have risked all kinds of vulnerability for that and I still would have felt like I'd accomplished something artful, even if the book hadn't been published and hadn't been read outside of my family.

Please don't call me a liar

I worry about being disavowed publicly. I worry about someone in my family calling me a liar. I worry about the way each of us remembers things differently and how some people take the way they remember things as the singular truth. I worry about alienating my relatives. I would rather have relatives than a book.

I also worry about treading that line too closely between

telling *my* truth as I know it and not offending members of my family. So in my memoir I wrote in disclaimers like, We remember this moment differently. I try to tell my version, but if others object to it, I tell their versions, too. I think it's important to acknowledge that just because you're the person writing the book, the person telling the public story, you're not saying yours is the only version, the final version.

I worry about imposing my published and better-known version of a communal history on others. It's very important to me that that subjectivity is acknowledged.

My story is your story

I aspire to tell my own version of the "truth" and to make it clear that it's my truth and mine alone. I aspire to create a work of art that can stand the test of time. I aspire to write something that tells a much bigger story than mine but uses my individual story as a vessel for a larger understanding of whatever I'm writing about.

I aspire to write something that people can read and feel deeply about. I don't want people to read my memoir and think they're eavesdropping on my therapy session. I want my story to be an engaging story that just happens to have happened to someone they may not know at all when they start to read the work but feel like they've known all their lives when they're done reading.

I'll be considerate, but I won't be silenced

I will compromise to a certain extent to take into consideration other people's feelings, but I will not be silenced. I think once you commit to a subject, some passion has driven you to it and that passion eventually calms your fears. I never censor myself while I'm writing. I remind myself that I don't have to publish everything I write. If you write the most honest first draft you can, I think that opens some pathways to better writing. Even if I take some things out later in the editing process, initially I write *everything*. The act of writing uncensored and freely for myself makes whatever ends up out in the world a lot more honest in the end.

When I was done with my memoir, I asked my brothers to read it. I told them to tell me if there was anything they objected to. Our father had just died and I didn't want to upset them further. They didn't object to anything so I kept it as is.

I learned this the hard way early on. Once I wrote something about a family member that seemed rather innocuous and it upset her a lot. I didn't want that to happen with my memoir. I am not sure what kinds of rewrites would have been involved if my brothers, for example, had asked me to remove them from the book. But I think I would have tried to respect their wishes because there was other material I could have pulled on to fill the gap.

It might have been different if something brutal had happened to me, for example, that they were denying. But it was innocuous enough that I wanted to consider their stories, which also added another layer to my father's story, which was something we all shared.

But I write what I want to write first and if I think it will upset folks close to me, I let them see it first. I understand you can't do that in journalism. This is probably why I'm not a journalist. My rule is, if you can reach the person and ask permission, you should at least try, especially if you're inserting them into your story in a way they might not like. Sometimes in spite of all your best efforts, you will inevitably break your own rules and cross certain boundaries. It's important to forgive yourself for that and keep writing.

Memoir is interactive

The best experience I've had as a memoirist is when people randomly talk to me about some personal moment of my life, which I forgot that I had written about in my memoir. Right before I open my mouth to ask how they know about that, I realize that they must have read it in my book.

When that happens, it feels as though we've gone through something together, or that we'd been present at the same event or events, when actually we had not. Those moments feel kind of magical to me, especially when people ask about some relative of mine and I'm, like, "How did you know so-and-so?" and the person says, "I read your book."

Writing an honest memoir is hard. And it's worth it

The writing itself can be hard. Writing in my memoir about the way my uncle died was tough because his death was so unjust and unnecessary. He was an eighty-one-year-old man who spoke with a voice box, and some immigration officers took away his medication and sent him to immigration jail, and when he got sick they accused him of faking.

I was able to get the records from my uncle's time in custody from the immigration service. I incorporated those records into my memoir. To relive both my uncle's and my father's last days was hard.

Looking over the documents detailing my uncle's ordeal and death was extremely hard. It is hard unearthing painful things in order to write your memoir. But you have to let yourself do it in order to reach that place where it's about more than just your own experience, where it grows into something larger than yourself. Where it becomes so transcendent that people who have had nothing like your experience can actually see themselves in what you've written.

What got me through this tough project was knowing that something better was going to come out of it—something like a piece of art or a memorial to my loved ones, something I could dip into later on and experience in a less painful way.

Don't do it for the money

Market forces had nothing to do with my writing a memoir.

It's not like fiction where you can, even if foolishly, plan for the market and tell yourself, I'm going to write dystopia because that's the genre that's in. You can't suddenly become a vampire to write a memoir about it. Or maybe you can. But with memoir you're dealing with a certain set of facts and you can share only what you have or what you're willing to go out and put yourself through. I've written one memoir and shorter works of nonfiction after that. I've written a travelogue and an essay collection, in which I talk about certain aspects of my life. I have a series of fictional volumes I could write, but not enough material for more memoirs. At least not yet.

I think of myself as a person who has written a memoir, rather than as a "memoirist." I think Maya Angelou is a great memoirist, for example. Mary Karr, too. Their lives are the subject of their work.

Write your own rules

Memoir requires its own kind of morality. And the only person who can police that morality is the writer, who develops a series of codes, guiding the personal choices that she or he is making.

People who are thinking of writing memoir should ask themselves where they would draw the line, whatever the line is. Would you feel comfortable exposing someone close to you to scrutiny that might change their entire lives? How much of yourself do you feel comfortable exposing?

Once you've written your no-holds-barred draft, your own series of rules about how far you're willing to go should be part of the rewrite or revision process.

Edwidge Danticat's Wisdom for Memoir Writers

- Don't mistake writing memoir for writing in your diary. You still have to write scenes and be engaging. You have to edit mercilessly, get rid of the extra stuff to move the narrative along. Don't just put things in because "they happened."

- Pause and reflect on the writing process itself. Make it real. Feed your senses. Go back to the place you're writing about. Do some research that allows you to bring your subject(s) to life.

- Respect your readers. Don't try to pull the wool over their eyes. Trust the actual story you have and trust the person who picks it up to read it in the genre you've indicated. If you're stretching the boundaries between what actually happened and your imagination, let the reader know.

- Writing memoir requires extra diligence. Sometimes you have to fact-check your memory against actual events to make sure you're on point. You might not always catch every mistake, but it's worth the effort to try.

CHAPTER SEVEN

Meghan Daum

*For more than twenty years now I have been making
something of a specialty of writing about myself. I still have
mixed feelings about the whole genre. In some respects,
serving as my own main subject has been a great
convenience. It saves me money on travel, research fees, and
even potential litigation (I cannot sue myself for libel, though
once or twice I've imagined confronting myself at a party,
asking, "How could you say those things!" and throwing a
drink in my face).*

—Opening, *The Unspeakable*, 2014

The roster of writers whose work is nearly unanimously ap-
preciated, respected, and beloved by publishers, book and
magazine editors, booksellers, critics, and readers is a short one
indeed. Even shorter list? Writers who earn that level of regard
right from the start of their careers.

Meghan Daum is an exception to that exception and no
wonder: her work is, in a word, exceptional. A Vassar graduate,
she was still a student in the MFA program at Columbia University's School of the Arts when she found her way onto the
pages of prestigious publications ranging from *The New York*

Times Book Review to *GQ*. "Things started clicking almost immediately," she wrote in *The Believer* in 2012, "and a central theme emerged: the relationship between myself and society, the tension between the trappings of contemporary life and the actualities of that life, what it meant to be 'alive' (i.e., twenty-five years old) in 'today's world' (i.e., New York City)."

Before you could say "Much like Joan Didion" (and several reviewers did), Meghan's incisive, intimate essays had earned her the moniker "voice of her generation." The personal essay, Meghan told the *Guardian*, allows her "to use [her]self as a vehicle to get into the layers of a subject . . . [which] has to be something universal."

Meghan Daum has the memoirist's gift for transforming the sow's ear of quotidian experience into one literary silk purse after another. The massive debt she'd accumulated by her early twenties sparked a *New Yorker* essay, "My Misspent Youth," which in turn became a book with that title. Her move to Nebraska in 1999, in part a result of her underwater New York City life, yielded a novel. And her musings on being an "honorary lesbian," an unabashed Joni Mitchell devotee, a survivor of a medical near-death experience, a not-mother-by-choice, and a less-than-storybook daughter begot her latest and greatest collection, *The Unspeakable*.

THE VITALS

Birthday: February 13, 1970

Born and raised: Born in California, raised in Texas and New Jersey

Home now: Los Angeles, California

Family: Married to *Los Angeles Times* reporter Alan Zarembo

Schooling: BA from Vassar College; MFA from Columbia University

Steady gig: Columnist for the *Los Angeles Times*

Notable notes:
- Meghan's column has run on the op-ed page of the *Los Angeles Times* since 2005.
- Meghan volunteers as a foster child advocate.
- You might have heard her voice on NPR's *This American Life*, *Morning Edition*, and/or PRI's *Marketplace*.
- *Slate* and *Entertainment Weekly* both named *The Unspeakable* a Top 10 Book of 2014.

Facebook: https://www.facebook.com/pages/Meghan-Daum /44319076324

Twitter: @meghan_daum

Website: www.meghandaum.com

THE COLLECTED WORKS

Memoirs/Essays

My Misspent Youth, 2001

Life Would Be Perfect If I Lived in That House, 2010

The Unspeakable, 2014

Fiction

The Quality of Life Report, 2003

Anthology

Selfish, Shallow, and Self-Absorbed: Sixteen Writers on the Decision Not to Have Kids, 2015

Essays, Articles, Reviews (Partial Listing)

The New Yorker

The New York Times

Harper's

GQ

Vogue

Meghan Daum

Why I write about myself

I write memoir when I feel there are no other options. Given the choice to write a first-person, memoiristic piece or, say, a profile of someone really interesting or a piece of cultural criticism, I'd pick either of the latter two any day (or most days). But for some reason, people seem to have a special affinity for my first-person work. I get asked to do it a lot.

By "no other options," I mean that when I want to go really deeply into a topic, and I want to do it right, I sometimes feel I have no choice but to mine my own history and experience. I can't research or report or interview my way around it. I have to open my own vein.

While that can be extremely challenging, memoir is still an inherently slacker-friendly form. The nature of readers' appetites and the pace of media these days has made it so that a lot of writers can kind of just skip the hard work and say, "Hey, look what happened to me!" or "Hey, I was a real screwup!" and not go any further than that.

Lazy memoirists, lazy editors, lazy readers

Lazy editors like to publish this sort of thing because there's less research and fact-checking involved, which is to say less liability. They can slap it online and watch the comments and page views pile up.

Readers then find that they're in the game less for a literary or educational experience than out of prurient interest or some kind of desire for a therapeutic experience. So you've got this cycle of lazy writers producing material for lazy editors to sell to lazy readers.

I realize I'm being cynical and grouchy, and maybe not entirely fair. There are some outstanding memoirs out there, and there are certainly ways of writing them that are anything but lazy or solipsistic. But this is a rare art. And it's one I'm still learning myself.

Personal essays versus memoir

I see myself as a personal essayist more than a memoirist. I know that distinction may seem negligible, but it's important to my work life and the way I go about conceiving projects.

To me, a personal essay is a piece in which I use my own experiences as a lens to look at larger, more universal issues and phenomena. It's just an essay, not an entire book. I guess it's the journalist in me, but when working in the first person I like the idea of writing a set of discrete pieces rather than a whole book. It's just more manageable for me.

My last collection of essays, *The Unspeakable*, was composed entirely of essays that hadn't been published elsewhere before. The pieces were written for that book and meant to be in the company of one another. Some people asked me why I didn't just write a straight-through book addressing the ideas that run through the essays. I'd considered that at one point, since it's a lot more palatable to publishers.

Ultimately it seemed right to do them as individual pieces. They each have their own unique arc and structure and tone, which is intended to take the focus away from Meghan, the narrator, and direct it toward something broader and more interesting. On her own, Meghan, the narrator, is not all that interesting.

I did write a straight-through memoir called *Life Would Be Perfect If I Lived in That House*. It was somewhat painful to do. I had to create connective tissue between the chapters, and that connective tissue sometimes felt superfluous. Without the natural breaks supplied by the essay format, you just kind of have to go on and on about yourself in ways that sometimes feel more like gristle than meat.

If you're a child soldier from Sierra Leone or a fourteen-year-old Olympic champion or some other kind of person who has a jaw-dropping, mesmerizing story, that's one thing. But I'm a middle-class white chick with no outsized childhood traumas or unusual accomplishments. My life story on its own isn't enough. So I need to be trafficking in external ideas as well as my own timeline.

Revealing myself makes me queasy

The way I feel before I've written about myself could be characterized as a combination of excitement and queasiness. When you have things you feel strongly about saying, there's an urgency about getting them on the page. But then, of course, writing can be loathsome and there are a million reasons to avoid it.

During the writing, if it's going well, I feel kind of pleasantly buzzed—anxious about finishing, worried that it's no good but also, at times, undeservedly optimistic about its quality. After the writing, especially when it's an early draft, I start wondering what my first readers are going to think.

Like most writers, I show early versions of my work to a few people. And although these people almost always make useful, sometimes invaluable suggestions, it can be devastating when they don't totally love the material right off the bat. I don't think there's a writer in the world for whom the words "This is a good start" don't make them want to punch the person who said it in the face.

I don't want to hurt anyone. Including me

What do I worry about? Everything.

If I'm writing a personal piece, I worry about people being upset or hurt by it. I try to soften any potential blows by implementing the old "be twice as hard on the narrator as you are on everyone else" trick. Just for good measure, I'm usually four times as hard on the narrator. But that doesn't change the fact that some people aren't going to get what you're trying to do, or won't take it in the spirit in which you intended it, or will otherwise feel violated in some way.

I worry that someone will be angry, that I'll violate a boundary, that I'll get something wrong. To maintain privacy, I almost always change names. Obviously if you're working in a formal journalistic capacity, it's not cool to change names unless there's a very clear reason for it, like the personal safety of the person you're writing about. You have to be completely transparent with the reader. You have to literally say, "X, who did not want his name to be used for Y reason."

In memoir or personal essay, you're not making that kind of contract with the reader. You're setting out to do work that's factual but also infused with acts of imagination. That doesn't give you license to make stuff up, but it does mean you can use certain flourishes or stylistic techniques that are more common in fiction.

Often, if I don't want to use someone's real name, I'll do something like "The doorman, who I'll call Paul . . ." In terms of including certain personal details about people, it's really a case-by-case judgment call. If a detail is potentially hurtful or sensitive in any way, I'll bend over backwards to leave it out and keep it in only if it's directly servicing the material.

I'm also conscious of which stories are mine to tell and which stories belong to other people. If I tell a story involving someone else, I make sure to tell it from my point of view. I make sure to tell it so it's a different story from the one the person would tell about himself. Otherwise, I'd just be stealing his story.

There's a story about my brother that is so fantastic and that I've always wanted to write or tell onstage. It has all the elements of a great yarn—absurdity, nostalgia, tragedy, desperation, an unbelievable twist followed by an even more unbelievable twist. But it's his story to tell, not mine. So even though he's unlikely to tell it, at least in public, I've kept my hands off of it. Grrr . . .

Hands off me, too

There are certain topics about myself that I've never taken on and have no immediate plans to write about. That may or may not change in the future. But for now they're off-limits, which means by definition that I can't tell you what they are.

So in some ways I inhibit myself. But that's not necessarily a bad thing. The world doesn't need to know everything about every one of us. In fact, one thing about some of us is probably more than enough.

Intimacy without oversharing

To me, writing personal narrative nonfiction should be an act of generosity toward the reader.

It's an invitation. The writer is saying to the reader, "Come along with me while I tell you a few things and explore a few ideas." The writer is saying, "Come a little closer and I'll confide in you about a few things."

The hope is those confidences will inspire the reader to unearth some of his own feelings or insights. None of this has to do with spilling your guts or handing your whole, unedited and unprocessed life story over to the reader to digest. That's just bad manners, bad hostessing. When you write about yourself—actually, when you write about anything—the goal is to offer up just the right ingredients in just the right portions. You're not dumping out the contents of the pantry. You're serving up a finished meal.

Good reading for good writing

Reading an amazing piece of writing inspires me to try to do something half as good. To read a piece of writing that presents its material in a way I didn't know was possible, or takes on a subject that never occurred to me before—that can put a spring in my step.

I also love having conversations with people who feel really passionately about something yet can't quite put their fingers on what it is—"This thing, it's been bothering me, it's been obsessing me, and I'm not sure why." That can make me want to go home and take a crack at an essay. I'll want to try to figure out what that thing is.

Sometimes the essay will start off in a very personal way. Sometimes it'll start as simply as, "Recently some friends and I were sitting around talking about X and we all realized we were utterly confused." That won't necessarily stay in there; plus, that's a very bland sentence. But the personal way into the piece is often a useful way to start.

You never know where the land mines are

Some of the best experiences I've had so far as a memoirist are happening right now.

My book *The Unspeakable* came out a few months ago. Before publication, I was extremely worried about a handful of the essays. There's a rawness and brutality in many of them that I wasn't sure would go down well with everyone.

Wait. Let me rephrase that. I *knew* they wouldn't go down well with everyone. More than that, I was afraid that lots of people would be just totally appalled. I'm talking especially about an essay called "Matricide," which is about the death of my mother and about the terrible relationship she had with her own mother, who died the same year she did, and also the complicated relationship she had with me. It's about the least sugar-coated, least "chicken soup for the soul" piece of writing you can imagine. It is not, for the most part, a flattering portrait of my mother and it's an even less flattering portrait of me. I very seriously considered not publishing it and, when I did, I was ready to be pilloried.

To my surprise, people seem genuinely moved by the piece and have been e-mailing me in droves thanking me for writing it. I even heard from someone who had been a friend of my mother's. He told me the essay was very moving to him and it made him think about his fraught relationship with his own mother. This was extraordinary to me because I knew that many of my mother's friends would be upset or even devastated by this essay—understandably so. But the fact that this man was able to get something out of it that had nothing to do with his friendship with my mother, that he was able to separate his experience of her from the experience of reading the essay, that was just breathtaking to me. In a single e-mail, this reader encapsulated the entire reason that I write personal narrative. I'll be forever grateful.

What sells versus what wants to be written: no contest

Market forces should probably affect me more than they do. So far, they've affected me not at all, which is evident in my bank balance. When I told my agent I wanted to write a book of original essays about things like death, not wanting children, and "phantom butchery" among other obscurities, she hardly had dollar signs flashing in her eyes. But I proceeded anyway and the book is finding its way to its audience.

I don't expect to get rich doing this. That's never been the intent and if it ever became the intent I'd be in trouble. Mostly I'm just grateful to be able to support myself as a writer at all. It may not get me the traditional trappings of a "privileged" life, but it's an incredible privilege to be able to do it.

Think you know me? Think again

It might surprise readers to learn they know a lot less about me than they probably think they do.

Unless your story is so over-the-top that you could tell it in a monotone and keep everyone riveted, there's a certain level of drama that you impose on that "I" narrator in order to engage the reader for any sustained period of time. For a relatively ordinary person like me, it helps to turn the volume up a notch or two—make yourself a little more neurotic, a little more intense, a little grouchier or more indignant. I'm not quite as neurotic and frenzied in real life as I might appear to be on paper. I'm probably a lot more boring than my work suggests.

Write like everyone you know is dead

As Joan Didion said, "Writers are always selling someone out." This can be true of reporting a newspaper article or writing a memoir.

When you're starting out on something, just go for it. Don't imagine negative Internet comments or how much you might upset your parents. Write like you're the sole survivor of a global apocalypse and it's your job to recall your life story as honestly and uncompromisingly as possible. (Okay, maybe there's another survivor, one who happens to be an editor at *The New Yorker*.)

I can't tell you how many students have written lackluster memoirs for my class, only to come to my office hours and unleash the most amazing stories. "But I can't write that," they'll tell me. "Oh, yes, you can," I'll say. Because here's the thing about safe, unprovocative material that you're not afraid of anyone reading: quite often, no one wants to read it anyway.

It can be a smart move to write memoirs in which many of the key players are dead, which might be less trouble if not inherently more moral. Some of my favorite memoirs, like Tobias Wolff's *This Boy's Life* and Joyce Johnson's *Minor Characters*, wisely take advantage of that. It also helps to come from a family that doesn't mind being written about or even gets a kick out of it, which unfortunately has not been the case with me.

That thing I said earlier about weighing each detail to determine whether it's worthy of inclusion? That's for the third, fourth, or fifth draft. Not the first draft.

The "morality" of any given project has to be evaluated on a case-by-case basis. If you're writing about yourself just for the sake of writing about yourself, and other people are going to get dragged along for the hellish ride, it might be wise to examine the worthiness of the venture. If you have something important to say that can only—or at least most effectively—be said through the lens of your own story, then go for it.

But go mindfully into the night. Every step of the way, ask yourself, Does this need to be in here? What purpose is this serving? If something is in there solely for the purpose of humor or entertainment, that's perfectly fine—if it's funny and entertaining enough to be worth it.

Bring something new

If you want to write funny stories about dating or parenting or your dysfunctional childhood, that's great. But in order to be successful doing that, you have to be really, really good (and really, really, really lucky). Why? Because just about everyone has funny stories about those things.

Do you know why readers love authors like Atul Gawande and Oliver Sacks and Ishmael Beah? Because they bring something new to the table. They tell their personal stories in the context of very specific worlds that they are uniquely qualified to bring to you.

So if you're reading this and you're in college or planning to go to college, consider that you don't even necessarily have to major in English to be a writer. Learn about medicine or sports or fashion or trapeze artists or Tibetan monks—anything other than your own navel.

Meghan Daum's Wisdom for Memoir Writers

- Become an expert at something other than yourself. Don't spend all your time in writing workshops; go out and learn about what interests you most and become the "go-to person" when it comes to your topic. Eventually editors will call you before you call them.
- Worry about other people's feelings—later. When you're writing your first draft, don't imagine negative Internet comments or how much you might upset your parents. Don't overthink it.
- Take most advice with a grain of salt, including mine. In literature, as in life, most advice says more about the giver than the receiver. So always consider the source. And if they're good ones, don't forget to thank them in your acknowledgments.

CHAPTER EIGHT

Nick Flynn

*All hushed, seven of us huddle in a kitchen, stare into a
monitor. It's about to start. The actress playing my mother
(Julianne Moore) stares back at us—she's in the middle of a
living room, the room is just behind this wall, but I haven't
gone into the living room, not yet. A set of headphones hangs
from an empty chair with my name on them—Dan points to
them, points to my head. It's only the sixth day of shooting,
we are in a house in Queens, the owner rents it out at times
for films like this, films that contain flashbacks to 1970s
smalltown America.*

—Opening, *The Reenactments*, 2013

Nick Flynn's father was a deluded alcoholic petty criminal
who abandoned Nick and his mother and spent several
years of Nick's childhood in prison. Paterfamilias Flynn also
believed that he was one of the three greatest writers in American
history. There was, according to Jonathan Flynn, Mark
Twain, and there was J. D. Salinger, and then there was Jonathan
Flynn. He shared these thoughts with his son in letters he
wrote from prison.

"Mostly they were deluded, but occasionally they were profound and filled with insight," Nick has said, "advice on how to be a writer, even though he knew nothing about me and didn't know I wanted to be a writer."

When Nick was twenty-two, his mother committed suicide. Two years later, he got a job at a homeless shelter in Boston. "I was young and lost and grieving," he says. "I'm not sure why working at a homeless shelter made sense to me, except that part of me knew that I needed to immerse myself in something larger than myself, if only to get out of the cage of my mind."

Three years later, his father showed up at the shelter—on the receiving end of the services Nick and his colleagues were administering. "It's hard enough to pick up somebody you don't know from the streets, but to have to pick your own father up—it was psychically devastating."

That experience was the impetus for his first bestselling memoir, *Another Bullshit Night in Suck City*, which was later adapted into the movie *Being Flynn*, with Robert De Niro playing Flynn's father.

"I became an electrician after high school," Nick says. "I wanted to be able to pay my rent. But I always had this thing in me to write. In my world, to say you were a poet was to say you were unreliable and more than likely a little crazy. I carried that sense around for a long time—for all I know it might be true."

THE VITALS

Birthday: January 26, 1960

Born and raised: Scituate, Massachusetts

Home now: Brooklyn, New York

Family: Married to Lili Taylor; daughter, Maeve Flynn

Schooling: Scituate High School; University of Massachusetts, Amherst; MA, New York University

Day job: Creative writing teacher at the University of Houston

Notable notes:
- Nick began his career as a poet with a seven-month poetry fellowship at the Fine Arts Work Center in Provincetown, Massachusetts.
- Nick is married to actress Lili Taylor.
- His awards and prizes include the 2005 PEN/Martha Albrand Award for the Art of the Memoir, a 2001 Guggenheim Fellowship, and the 1999 PEN/Joyce Osterweil Award for Poetry.

Facebook: https://www.facebook.com/nick.flynn1?fref=ts

Twitter: @_nick_flynn_

Website: www.nickflynn.org

THE COLLECTED WORKS

Memoirs

Another Bullshit Night in Suck City, 2004

The Ticking Is the Bomb, 2010

The Reenactments, 2013

Poetry

Some Ether, 2000

Blind Huber, 2002

The Captain Asks for a Show of Hands, 2011

My Feelings, 2015

Plays

Alice Invents a Little Game and Alice Always Wins, 2008

Nonfiction

A Note Slipped Under the Door (coauthored with Shirley McPhillips), 2000

Essays, Articles, Reviews, Etc.

The New Yorker

The Paris Review

The New York Times Book Review

This American Life

Film Collaborations

Darwin's Nightmare, 2004

Being Flynn, 2012

Nick Flynn

Why I write about myself

I don't usually know what form something will take when I begin writing. I don't even really begin. I write every day, and once in a while something begins to take shape, begins to have a form. Sometimes that form seems to be more prose than poetry or drama or . . .

I don't know if there's anything distinct about the urge to write memoir beyond the urge I have to write, period.

If you look at *Suck City*, you might notice that there are several different forms woven together: plays, lists, performance pieces, letters, documents. Some of the passages are so lyrical they read closer to poetry. Some contain more of what might be called "grounding energy." I can say that it wasn't clear until the eleventh hour which of these moving parts would fit into the final form, so each was evolving until the moment it landed.

I try to come to the edge of what I know and push a little further over that edge. I think that any topic or scene or action that elicits any of the "lesser" emotions—shame, guilt, humiliation, etc.—is likely where the good stuff is lurking. I try to go there, and I try to bring the reader along on that journey.

Compassion, not self-protection

I try to have compassion for everyone who ends up in my books, even myself. But I don't consciously think about protecting myself, or presenting myself as either victim or hero, because it seems to me that part of the job description is to push into these unfamiliar, uncomfortable psychic terrains.

That said, I am aware that I really have no access to anyone else's inner psychic terrain, and the moments I drift there, trying to imagine my father's inner life, say, I know I am in the realm of fiction. The best I can hope for is to try to write toward a compassionate understanding of whoever ends up in the books—often one I might not have been able to achieve when they were in my life.

Why memoir matters

A memoir is not simply stringing together the five or ten good stories you've been telling about your wacky childhood for your whole life. To cross the threshold into the deeper mysteries, you need to ask yourself why you've been telling those particular stories, and not the millions of others you could tell. Memoirs that are worth reading are memoirs that address these difficult questions.

I can name several writers who go there. Kelle Groom. Stephen Elliott. Sarah Manguso. Rebecca Solnit. Eula Biss. Leslie Jamison. Anthony Swofford. Christa Parravani. Maggie Nelson. Joshua Cody. Claudia Rankine. Andrew Meredith. Wayne Koestenbaum. Jacqueline Woodson. This list is incomplete, top of my head, but you get the idea. These are memoirs that are engaged with some of the deepest and most difficult questions of what it is to be alive at this moment.

Walter Benjamin offers this, which perhaps says it better than I can: "It is half the art of storytelling to keep a story free from explanation as one reproduces it . . . The most extraordinary things, marvelous things, are related with the greatest accuracy, but the psychological connection of the events is not forced on the reader. It is left up to him to interpret things the way he understands them, and thus the narrative achieves an amplitude that information lacks."

Don't play God; observe

One thing that interests me about working in this genre is the tension built into trying to get the facts of this world accurate to the best of my ability. Not to play God with the world, but to observe it as clearly as possible, and then to allow my subjective inner world to filter what I believe I am seeing, to interpret it, as best I am able, in the hope that it might reveal something of my inner landscape.

I like what Mary Gaitskill once said, answering an interviewer who said he didn't know what to feel about the characters in her novel *Veronica*: "You don't know what to feel? You're an adult, you feel what you feel."

Nick Flynn's Wisdom for Memoir Writers

- There are always stories to tell. But to justify a memoir, there has to be a good reason to tell it.
- I think this Mary Gaitskill quote should be pinned over the desk of anyone who is writing a memoir: "It's not my job as an artist to tell you what to feel."
- It's all about how well the memoir is written. It's all in the syntax.

CHAPTER NINE

A. M. Homes

I remember their insistence that I come into the living room
and sit down and how the dark room seemed suddenly
threatening, how I stood in the kitchen doorway holding a
jelly doughnut and how I never eat jelly doughnuts.

I remember not knowing; first thinking something was very
wrong, assuming it was death—someone had died.

And then I remember knowing.

—Opening, *The Mistress's Daughter*, 2007

⌢⌣

A. M. Homes is a novelist. A short story writer. A memoirist. A journalist. A TV screenwriter. A creative writing lecturer. An art historian and art critic. A recipient of several of the world's most prestigious writing prizes.

But the description that's most inextricably linked to A. M. Homes and her fearless, iconoclastic, disturbing writing is "controversial." A *Tin House* interviewer nailed it, calling Homes "a social arsonist."

"What I'm doing, which sometimes makes people uncomfortable, is saying the things we don't often say out loud,"

Homes commented in 2013, when her seventh novel, *May We Be Forgiven*, won the vaunted Baileys Women's Prize (formerly the Orange Prize) for Fiction. "When people say they're shocked by something, it just means I hit a nerve."

That's a good thing for those who admire Homes's "shocking" work—for example, her 1996 novel *The End of Alice*, written from the point of view of an imprisoned child molester who's coaching a nineteen-year-old girl on the best way to seduce a twelve-year-old boy. Michael Cunningham said the book "establishes A. M. Homes as one of the bravest, most terrifying writers working today. She never plays it safe, and it begins to look as if she can do almost anything."

In this one way, at least, Homes is like many New York writers (and New Yorkers): her work was profoundly affected by the 9/11 attack, which she watched from her living room windows. "It made me think a lot about our responsibilities to and for each other," she said, "and to reconsider how one can live optimistically in a time that is inherently not optimistic."

This A. M. Homes fan finds all of her work fundamentally optimistic. What could be more hopeful than to trust that one's readers will find the humanity in the kinds of difficult, important stories she tells?

THE VITALS

Birthday: December 18, 1961

Born and raised: Washington, DC

Home now: New York, New York

Schooling: Sarah Lawrence College; Iowa Writers' Workshop; Whitney Museum of American Art Independent Study Program

Day job: Nope

Notable notes:

- *Jack*, Homes's first novel, was written as homework when she was nineteen.
- Homes was a writer/producer for seasons two and three of *The L Word*.
- She's the recipient of fellowships from the Guggenheim Foundation, the National Endowment for the Arts, the New York Public Library, the National Foundation for the Arts, the Cullman Center for Scholars and Writers, and the New York Foundation for the Arts.

Facebook: https://www.facebook.com/profile.php?id=63000 6933&fref=ts

Twitter: @nycnovel

Website: www.amhomesbooks.com

THE COLLECTED WORKS

Novels

Jack, 1989

In a Country of Mothers, 1993

The End of Alice, 1996

Appendix A:, 1996

Music for Torching, 1999

This Book Will Save Your Life, 2006

May We Be Forgiven, 2012

Essays, Columns (Partial Listing)

The New Yorker

Artforum

Vanity Fair

McSweeney's

Bomb

Granta

Nonfiction

Los Angeles, 2002

The Mistress's Daughter, 2007

Story Collections

The Safety of Objects, 1990

Things You Should Know, 2002

A. M. Homes

Why I write about myself

With the exception of the one memoir, which is more about my biological parents, I don't do that very often—I don't like writing about myself.

I mostly work from my imagination. My novels aren't autobiographical, or even drawn closely from my own experience. People often tell writing students, "Write what you know." I come at it from the opposite school, which is "Write what you don't know."

It was tough, deciding to write the memoir. In 2004 I published a *New Yorker* piece about meeting my biological parents for the first time in my thirties. A variety of things moved me to complete the book. The first was the impulse to organize the information and the experience—to put it in a container, if only to set the container aside for a while.

I was aware of the way things shift as time passes—circumstances change; people die—and your relationship to past experience and history also shifts. I wanted to capture the story in as close to its original essence as I could.

Having an *impulse* to write a book was in itself a new thing for me. I *never* have the impulse to write a novel!

A big piece of my motivation was to research my history, both my adoptive and biological relatives whose lives I didn't know. I wanted to achieve some kind of understanding of them, and the kinds of decisions they'd made, and the time period in which my adoption happened. In that sense, I was still writing what I didn't know—while at the same time poking at something that was a very deep and very primitive wound, asking myself as I was doing it, "Hey! How does that feel?"

Writing memoir is not fun

Writing my memoir was unpleasant, like being a doctor examining myself: Does it hurt here? Which part hurts the most? Oops! I made you bleed again.

There were many points at which I thought, I don't really want to be doing this. I want to stop.

What propelled me to keep going was that I felt I could bring to the memoir my experience and training as a writer—finding language for primitive emotional experiences. One of the things that worked about the book was that it gave voice to people who hadn't found language for their adoption experience. It allowed them to explore their own experience in a different way, and/or to have their feelings about it articulated and confirmed.

You can't un-know what you know

The Mistress's Daughter is like a public service announcement. The message is "You can't hold off what you know."

This goes back to an idea that's true in my fiction as well. I firmly believe that there are things we already know and spend a lot of time resisting. You can try, but the amount of energy you spend trying not to know what you already know will be exhausting.

I grew up knowing I was adopted but not knowing who my biological parents were. Then, when I was in my thirties, my biological mother contacted the lawyer who'd handled the adoption and told him she was interested in meeting me. The lawyer contacted my adoptive parents, and they had to decide whether to tell me. They did.

I wasn't who I thought I was, and yet I didn't know who I was. It was interesting to realize how fragile your identity is. Even when you're thirty-something years old, and you've written a bunch of books, and you think you know who you are, the reveal of a piece of information, an addition or subtraction to your known narrative, can yank it all out from under you.

I had to decide whether I was going to allow this experience of "being found" in, and how I would assimilate it. I knew it would upset my sense of self, my identity. Through the lawyer, I asked my biological mother, "Who was my father?" That question brought both my biological parents into my life. They weren't a couple. My father was and is married to the woman he'd been married to all along. My parents' relationship had been ongoing for seven years before I was born. My birth ended it. It was like being drawn into the middle of an affair, but as an adult.

Being given up at birth is a pretty profound thing. And I was adopted into a family whose child had died at age nine. There was a lot of grief in the air. I liken it to growing up inside a Eugene O'Neill play.

Since publishing the memoir, the biggest personal shift is that I now feel a greater sense of legitimacy. I feel I have the right to be alive, the right to exist. I felt very peripheral as a kid; it was an uncomfortable way to live.

Form and content and form

There's a big difference between undergoing a personal exploration and writing a memoir about it.

As the story of my being found by my birth parents was unfolding, I made a lot of notes. I used those in the first half of the book, which is a fairly traditional personal account. In the second half, I took a very different approach. I looked at the story from a genealogical, anthropological point of view. In the process of researching my family history, I came across histories of hundreds of immigrants. It was incredibly interesting.

I never think about form ahead of time. I'd never presume to come up with a form in advance of the story. You need the story to dictate its own terms to you. When it does, why resist?

Once you've got the information you need, then you start shaping it into a book. That's one way in which writing memoir is very different from writing fiction. In nonfiction and memoir, the big thing is getting story right—staying true to the experiences, and the facts as you know them to be—the emotional truth of it all. Then comes form. With the memoir there were a couple of chapters that got very long, mostly the anthropological exploration. We got rid of it. It didn't serve the story. It was important to my process of figuring out what I was trying to do, but just because your experience takes you through twenty or thirty steps, that doesn't mean the reader needs to take those steps with you.

In some memoirs, those two things get confused: the experience the reader's going to have versus the story the author needs to explore. If you're going to publish a memoir, it needs to work as a book.

Guessing about the truth is fiction

I was very mindful of being accurate. When I came across something I wasn't sure of, I'd say, "I imagine that . . ." Or I'd note that it had the possibility of projection or imagination, instead of just saying it was true.

As someone who writes in both genres, I'm very aware of the difference between fiction and nonfiction. There's no doubt in my mind that a writer knows when they're making something up. You know when something's a fact, when it happened, and when it isn't. But there's been this weird blurring of fiction and nonfiction. People say, "It's hard to know what you remember." I say, "No, it's not!"

I'm a stickler for nonfiction being truly nonfiction. That was one of the hardest things for me as I was writing a memoir.

When you're writing a novel, you're thinking of the character. It's an organic evolution. With memoir, there's a very specific story you're trying to tell. You're trying to determine what happened, and when, and to whom.

Whenever I'm writing nonfiction, I try to stay close to what I know of the facts; to illuminate an experience that is not often described or available to people.

And actually, when I'm writing fiction I'm trying to do the same thing; to give language and understanding to an experience that may not be a familiar one to people—whether it's a jailed pedophile murderer, or a Nixon scholar who sleeps with his brother's wife. My personal mandate is always to tell the truth according to the character. That mandate came to me from my most influential teacher, Grace Paley. In memoir, unfortunately, the character is me. But that doesn't change my aspiration or my goal.

It always goes back to character and storytelling. If people want to define me as transgressive or shocking, all I can say is that none of that is of any relevance or interest to me. I'm trying to explore the lives of my characters as I understand them. That's also true of the memoir. I was trying to explore both my own relationship to the experience and also what I learned about all of my families.

Protecting characters cheats the truth

Early on in the writing, I realized I was being protective of my biological parents' identities. It was a very difficult decision to give that up. I felt that if I didn't tell the story as honestly as I could it would cheat the material. Protecting my biological par-

ents also meant I was agreeing that there was something to be
ashamed of. I thought, I can't do that to myself, or send that
message of "shame" to all the other people who have been in
pain because they were adopted or had given up a child or
adopted one.

I kind of came undone, struggling with what it would mean
to stop protecting the people I was writing about. On the one
hand, I was bringing attention to people who didn't ask for attention. On the other hand, if I didn't tell the story clearly, if I
hemmed and hawed, I'd be acting like being adopted was
something to be ashamed of—which meant that *I* was something to be ashamed of, and that's something I'd worked hard
to put behind me.

Whose story is it, anyway?

I didn't ask anyone's permission to tell the story the way I experienced it. I couldn't imagine saying, "Oh, by the way, you parents, teachers, formerly dearly beloveds who have had enormous
power over me my whole life, I want your permission to be
honest." There were a couple of details we took out because the
lawyer advised me to take them out, and I was fine with that.
They were interesting and revealing, but relatively minor in
terms of the overall story.

People were always asking me, "How can you write something like that?" The answer is, if it's true, you can say it. That's
the upside and the downside of writing memoir—it's painful,
and it's real.

I didn't need to ask my adoptive parents because, oddly
enough, the book isn't about them. On an artistic level, includ-

ing them would have made the scope of the book too big. I gave them the book to read very early on. My mother asked me to change one line, about my father being a leftist. That was it.

My mother was so proud of me, and of the book. I was really surprised by that. My parents live in Washington, DC, where the adoption took place and where my biological parents still live. It's one thing for me to have a life as a writer. It's another thing for people in my extended family to learn things they hadn't known before they read it in my memoir—like the fact that my biological parents had come looking for me.

I don't exactly regret this, but it's always an issue when I write about myself: there are people—whether it's my adoptive family or members of my biological family I'm not in touch with—who are shaken and upset by the material.

The most important thing is that I don't want to be ashamed of my existence. I don't want to lie about it. I didn't write the book to be hurtful to people, but the truth can be hurtful.

A memoir should do some good. And not just for the memoirist

When I was working on *The Mistress's Daughter*, other memoirists warned me that if I published it, everyone in the world would want to tell me their adoption stories. They were right, and I'm glad.

I find it incredibly touching when I'm doing a reading in New York or Australia or England and afterward people tell me the book has been there for them as a guide, that it's helped them find themselves, that they give the book to friends and family to show themselves to other people.

At one reading, a man in his eighties came up to me and told me his wife was adopted and she'd been trying to find her family. He said my book had helped both of them. Then the other day, a woman told me she'd given up a child and she was trying to find her. It was heartbreaking.

Controversy is not a bad thing

Before I wrote the memoir, I wrote multiple books that were banned or, at minimum, controversial. My first novel, *Jack*, is on hundreds of school reading lists and yet remains one of the one hundred most banned books in the country because it's about a kid whose dad is gay. *The End of Alice* was banned in England and took seventeen years to be published in France, and yet stories about child abuse are in every newspaper around the world—daily.

I think the first question a writer has to ask is, Do we run away from subject matter because it causes controversy? My answer, as author and activist, is a definite *no*. Then you bring the question closer to home: do you run away from controversy that would cause pain for people you care about? The answer is still no.

Everywhere I go, even before I wrote my memoir, people ask me if they're allowed to write their stories. I say write it, then decide afterward what to do with it.

This doesn't have anything to do with playing God. It's a simple fact of legitimacy. Do I have the right to tell the story of my existence? I have worked very hard to become the person I am—to be respected by others, to do all the things I do, many of them anonymously, to improve the lives of others. I'm not going to negate myself to protect someone's feelings.

I wrote *Jack* at age nineteen. The protagonist's dad was gay. When I wrote it, my teacher said, "This will be very controversial." I remember thinking, That's unfortunate.

It doesn't matter to me whether it's fiction or nonfiction. Making art is all about humans and our psychology: who we are, how we behave, what we do with the hand we've been dealt. It's closer to your own bone when it's a memoir, but the bone is still the bone.

A. M. Homes's Wisdom for Memoir Writers

- Write the most honest, truthful version of your story you can. That first draft is *your* draft. Don't run away from whatever comes up for you when you do. Explore it.

- There's a huge decision to make between writing a story and publishing it. Don't write with the assumption that you'll publish it; that's not why we write memoir. You're writing it to document your life and your story. If anything else comes of it, make decisions accordingly.

- With a memoir, as with a novel, the key is trying to understand what your "characters" saw and felt. Using the conventions of good storytelling—time, place, voice, dialogue—to illuminate a story is really important to moving the story along.

CHAPTER TEN

Sue Monk Kidd

*There was a time in Africa the people could fly. Mauma told
me this one night when I was ten years old. She said,
"Handful, your granny-mauma saw it for herself. She say
they flew over trees and clouds. She say they flew like
blackbirds. When we came here, we left that magic behind."*

—Opening, *The Invention of Wings*, 2014

Here's what makes *The Invention of Wings* extraordinary . . . :
Sue Monk Kidd has written a conversation changer. It is
impossible to read this book and not come away thinking differently about our status as women and about all the unsung heroines who played a role in getting us to where we are."

What makes this fan letter kind of extra-special is its author. That would be Oprah Winfrey, who loved *The Invention of
Wings* so much that she: (1) chose it for her Book Club 2.0 before she'd even finished reading the galleys; (2) devoted several
pages in *O, The Oprah Magazine* to an interview with Sue; (3)
interviewed Sue for an adoring hour on OWN TV's *Super Soul
Sunday*; and (4) bought the film rights to the book.

Oprah is not alone in her adoration. *The Invention of Wings*
wasn't Sue Monk Kidd's first foray into bestsellerdom. Her 2002

novel *The Secret Life of Bees* spent years on the *New York Times* list, was nominated for England's prestigious Orange Prize, and was made into an awarding-winning movie in 2008. *The Mermaid Chair* became a 2006 TV movie starring Kim Basinger.

Not bad for a woman who published her first novel at age fifty-three.

Sue Monk Kidd is a seeker and a teller of spiritual, gender, and racial truths, topics not always popular in American culture or in Sue's native South.

"I grew up amid the backdrop of separate water fountains, black maids riding in the back seats of white ladies' cars, Rosa Parks, and Civil Rights marches," Sue told an interviewer. "One of my earliest memories is seeing the Ku Klux Klan on the street in my small hometown in Georgia and the absolute terror I felt . . .

"I've been drawn to write about racial themes because they are part of me, and also because they matter deeply to me. I can't help but feel a social responsibility about it as a writer."

Meet Sue Monk Kidd, bestselling author, racial equality activist, and Southern belle-buster.

THE VITALS

Birthday: August 12, 1948

Born and raised: Sylvester, Georgia

Home now: Southwest Florida

Family: Husband Sanford Kidd; son Bob (1972); daughter Ann Kidd Taylor (1976); grandchildren Roxie (2003), Ben (2003), Max (2006)

Schooling: Texas Christian University, BS in nursing, 1970

Day job: Nope

Notable notes:

- Bees lived inside a bedroom wall of Sue Monk Kidd's childhood home in Georgia, becoming the inspiration for *The Secret Life of Bees.*
- After eight years as a nurse, at age thirty Sue started taking writing classes at the local college. Her first essay was published that same year. Her first nonfiction books were published in 1990 and 1996. She was fifty-three when her first novel was published.
- *The Secret Life of Bees* was not Sue's first book, but it was her first to hit the *New York Times* bestseller list, in 2002. It has since sold eight million copies in thirty-six countries.
- Her novels *The Mermaid Chair* and *The Invention of Wings* were both #1 *New York Times* bestsellers.

Facebook: https://www.facebook.com/suemonkkidd

Twitter: @suemonkkidd

Website: www.suemonkkidd.com

THE COLLECTED WORKS

Memoir

Traveling with Pomegranates (coauthored with Ann Kidd Taylor), 2009

Novels

The Secret Life of Bees, 2002

The Mermaid Chair, 2005

The Invention of Wings, 2014

Nonfiction

God's Joyful Surprise, 1988

When the Heart Waits, 1990

The Dance of the Dissident Daughter, 1996

Firstlight, 2006

Film Adaptations

The Mermaid Chair, 2006

The Secret Life of Bees, 2008

The Invention of Wings, in development

Sue Monk Kidd

Why I write about myself

One of my big fears is to be disconnected from my own story. It's like being unmoored from my life.

I started writing at age thirty. What drove me was the love of narrative. Truth be told, I wanted to write fiction. But I had the reality of a young family—a husband and two small children. I'd given up my career in nursing, and I needed to do something to make up that income, to help support the family. So I began freelancing, writing articles and essays. There was a necessity in that. But I discovered that a narrative that emerges from my own experience is very compelling to me—perhaps as much as a narrative from my imagination.

At the bottom of all memoir writing is the question, Who am I? and I suppose I was trying to figure that out. I'm cursed—and maybe a little blessed, too—by being very introspective. I'm constantly probing and contemplating my inner life. Oddly enough, I find that the deeper I go into myself, the more I'm freed from myself. When I write about myself, I find release and freedom in the end because I've managed to distill the experience into some sort of meaning that I can integrate into my life, and then move on without all the preoccupation and unconscious pull of it. It's the unexamined experience that seems to wreak the most havoc in my day-to-day world.

Writing memoir not only has the ability to reveal me to myself, it also has the power to change me. I suspect writing memoir is partially about the need to bring about wholeness in myself. Maybe I'm trying to resolve something inside, heal a wound, redeem some part of myself that has been orphaned or lost, or give a voice to what has been silenced. *The Dance of the Dissident Daughter* was the story of how my religion and spirituality collided into my feminism, and writing it changed me. It allowed me to recover something vital and true in myself. It made me a much braver person. I don't think I would've been able to write my first novel if I hadn't written that memoir.

At its best, writing draws from the inner life, from a place deep within where we are sourced. We could call it the life of the soul. This place is filled with so much genius—an ordinary genius that's common to us all. It's the room where our dreams and imagination live. It's where our wisdom lies, where memories are metabolized, images are born, and creative connections are made. I see it as an inner reservoir. I think there's even divinity in it—something beyond our egos and our conscious selves. I'm talking about the contemplative life, of course, which is, for me, a significant part of the writing life.

On the other hand, I don't want to mystify the process too much. Another significant part of writing is just plain hard work: sitting your behind in a chair and staying there.

Why I write

As a child, I wanted desperately to become a writer, but when it came time to go to college I chose nursing. It was 1966 in the prefeminist South. My decision to major in nursing was about being safe, being traditional. It was a failure of courage on my part—knowing that I wanted to be a writer but not finding my way to do that.

I ended up working as a nurse for eight years. I have the highest regard for the profession, but it wasn't my place. It took more courage than I felt I had for me to seize the thing I was meant to do, and that was writing.

Before I made the leap, I grew so restless. I had so much unfulfilled longing, so much pent-up creativity. I was working part-time as an RN on a pediatric unit. I had two toddlers, a husband, a brick house, and a station wagon. There's a line of poetry from Anne Sexton that I used as a chapter epigraph in *The Dance of the Dissident Daughter*: "One can't build little white picket fences to keep the nightmares out." It was sort of like that.

On my thirtieth birthday, I was in the laundry room when it all seemed to come to a head. I remember dumping a bunch of diapers into the machine—this was before I had the sense to splurge on disposables. I remember closing the lid, putting my hands on the washer as it started to vibrate, and thinking, I'm going to become a writer. I must do this, sink or swim. I marched right into the kitchen, where my husband was sitting with our two toddlers, who were eating their cereal, and I made my announcement, "I'm going to be a writer."

Of course, it took about five minutes before I thought,

What am I doing? Of course I can't write; I don't know any-thing about writing. I know now that this internal backlash of fear is often what comes when we step out there and do some-thing bold. But at the time I thought I must be insane.

Writing needs reading

It took ten years after that announcement for me to have a book published. I spent those years trying to discover my voice and my truth, as well as apprenticing myself to the craft of writing.

I enrolled in a creative writing class at a local college, joined a writers' group, and attended a stream of writing conferences. Honestly, though, the most significant thing I did was read vo-raciously. I'd always been a reader, but now I became a *reader.* I tried to read at the level at which I wanted to write. It was excruciating—the expectations I suddenly had, not to mention the gap between what I was reading on the page and what I was actually able to put on the page myself. It was overwhelmingly daunting. But I kept reading.

The book that had the biggest effect on me was *The Awak-ening,* by Kate Chopin. To this day the book sits on the desk where I write. I read Sylvia Plath, Eudora Welty, Toni Morri-son, Flannery O'Connor, Alice Walker, Virginia Woolf . . . I cried through *A Room of One's Own.* That book resonated so strongly with me. I also read a lot of spiritual books of a con-templative nature, the classics of contemplative literature, espe-cially the works of Thomas Merton. Eventually, I read C. G. Jung, whose works on the human psyche turned out to be a very powerful writing teacher.

There were all these little spiritual awakenings going on in me at the time. For me, creativity and spirituality are inherently linked. I can't really separate them. Authentic creativity is spiritual experience, and vice versa. There are so many things about writing that matter. But what always mattered the most to me was where it was sourced—where it came from.

The courage to be real

Finding courage may be the hardest thing about writing.

First I had to find the nerve to voice myself at all, to find that place in myself and follow it. Then it became about the courage to write authentically. To think and act outside of the confines of the world that shaped me, to express my own truth and my own voice.

I was ambitious right from the start. I wanted my work to be read. Of course, I still do. But what I've learned over the years is that what matters in the end is following my own thread, my own wellspring. That has to be enough for me.

There's often a tension between commercial success and being true to oneself as a writer. It's a useful tension, just like the tension I sometimes feel between believing utterly in what I'm doing and doubting it at same time. Somehow, that latter pull of opposites has always brought out the best in my work. I think the tension between commercial success and realizing an authentic vision is similar—it's a good paradox for a writer.

Success is a hard act to follow

My first novel sold millions of copies. Who wouldn't want that kind of readership? The only proper response is gratitude, and I feel that in every bone in my body. I still feel surprised that the whole thing happened. It changed everything. It threw me into a whole other arena. It brought a lot of wondrous things to my door.

But it also brought challenges. Like many writers, I'm an introvert. I love my solitude, the quietness of my study. And I happen to be very contemplative by nature. Then suddenly I'm out there. It was a very interesting time. It brought this whole new set of learning experiences.

Author persona versus the author, person

There's the compelling pull of what my readers expect and what my publisher wants and expects, which has sometimes led to anxiety about having to perform. It has been helpful to realize that I have a public self, this author persona I call "Sue Monk Kidd." And then there's this "writer me" who has a private heart.

When I write memoir, particularly, I'm writing out of my private heart. I insist that the public persona has to stay outside my study door. I don't always manage it, but I try. The most conflict I feel as a writer is probably between these two parts of myself—the public self and the private heart.

Write from the source . . .

I ultimately believe that when I write authentically from the source, and I'm true to that, it's not only good for my soul and my wholeness, it's good for my work. I have to believe that ultimately the work will prevail. It will find its way. It will find its audience. Even if what I set out to do morphs into something else, it will serve its purpose.

. . . even when it's terrifying

The scariest thing about writing memoir is the terrifying vulnerability of it. *Dissident Daughter* was the hardest of my books to write as far as mustering the courage to speak my truth. *Mermaid* was the hardest in terms of living up to expectations, but *Dissident Daughter* forced me to declare my truth in the most public way. I had to pull a pocket inside out, and there I was.

I often think of what poet David Whyte wrote: "Revelation must be terrible, knowing you can never hide your voice again." Writing memoir can feel like a unilateral disarmament. This must be what a lot of memoir writers feel—the exposure, the nakedness of it all. We're writing out of our private hearts, then putting it out there for everyone to look at. Of course that's terrifying!

The privacy factor

Revealing oneself, disarming in front of the reader, can create a relationship with the reader that's profoundly intimate.

The reader and the writer come together in a work. It's such a mystery. Much of that coming together has to do with the identification that the reader has with the writer, precisely because the writer was willing to be vulnerable, to say, "Here's my life as it is. Here are my doubts. My darkness."

I don't know why really, but I've been compelled to reveal myself on the page, yet when it comes to other people I'm more hesitant. If I seem to be cutting too close to the bone where they are concerned, I'll ask them about it. They'll usually say go ahead. It's a dance between being true to my need to write authentically and my responsibility to those around me not to cross over into their private hearts and extract something that doesn't belong to me.

Whenever I use someone's name or reference them, I send them the relevant page or pages of the manuscript before turning the book in. They are usually close friends or family members. I tell them, "This is what I'm saying; if you have problems with it, let's talk about it. I won't necessarily change the content, but I'll change your name."

No one has ever asked me to do that, although some people have corrected some of my facts, which I was very grateful for.

The common heart

Back when I first started writing, I took a graduate writing course at Emory University in which the teacher said something like, "The job of the writer is to serve her work." It made a big impression on me. When I turned fifty, I realized I'd pretty much spent most of my writing career focused on that, on serving my work. The burning issues were always about excellence and authenticity: How can I make my writing better, deeper, truer? Is it true to my voice and my vision? Questions like that often consumed me. They were vital; they still are. But as I got older, the point was not only how I served my work; it was about what my work served.

Of course, this was me getting older, having more years behind me than ahead of me. At fifty-seven, grandchildren began arriving in my life, and I was asking myself what legacy I would be leaving behind. I wanted to make my small dent in the world.

In the most general way, writing is about soul making for one individual writer, but I believe it can also be about making the soul of the world. Not to sound too high-minded about it, but writing can make a difference in the world around us.

In college, I became very big on Ralph Waldo Emerson. It was through his writings that I first came upon the phrase "the common heart." He described it as a place inside of us where we share an intrinsic unity with all humanity. That rang very true to me, and the notion stuck. I realized that writing memoir and fiction has the ability to offer readers a portal into the common heart. It gives them a way to take another's experience and make it their own. It gives them an experience of empathy, taking them into the common heart. That's an amazing thing, really, when you think about it.

I guess what I'm saying is that I want my writing to serve something larger than just myself.

Limiting exposure

I believe there's a limit to the vulnerability you should put out there when you write—your own and other people's. I'm much more careful with other people's privacy than I am with my own. There's a fine line between telling the truth and going for shock value. There's a discretion you use that's wise. Disclosing a private truth in order to shock the reader and garner sales, rather than to illuminate or serve the work, is a parameter that doesn't need to be crossed.

When I wrote *Dissident Daughter*, I was filled with this vast feeling of being a woman coming into myself. It was not without its conflicts. I had to consider my husband. I sat down and talked to him about it, and he said, "Just tell the truth." So I did. I told the truth of that experience, but I didn't have to put every detail in there.

When my kids were young, and I was writing a lot of personal experience articles about mothering, in which they prominently figured, I asked their permission because I didn't want to embarrass them with their friends. I'm their mom—I didn't want to do that to them. If they nixed it, I nixed it. I just think there's a time and place to be careful with how we use our work. There's such a thing as being overly revelatory.

Now that my kids are grown, I don't write about them anymore, though I did coauthor a memoir with my daughter, Ann. *Traveling with Pomegranates* was in part about the reinvention of our relationship. People would say to us, "You're writing a memoir together and you're still speaking?" We'd say, "Yep, we are." I was in my fifties and Ann was in her twenties when we had the experiences we wrote about, but we wrote it eight years later, long after we'd found a new intimacy as mother and daughter.

It took us three years to write the book. We did what I would call a really truthful collaboration. I had a quote by Anaïs Nin that I'd kept on my desk while I was writing *The Dance of the Dissident Daughter*, and I dug it out and copied it for Ann, and we both kept it on our desks while we were writing *Pomegranates*. It reads, "The role of a writer is not to say what we can all say, but what we are unable to say."

That's what Ann and I aspired to—not to say the obvious thing about being a mother and a daughter, but to say something deeper, to say what is hard to say. That's also what I'd tried to do with *Dissident Daughter*, and I think that's why the book was so controversial when it came out. In *Pomegranates*, Ann felt free to tell her truth, and I felt free to tell mine. We wrote about our conflicts, our failures and longings, about how we lost each other and how we found each other again, but in a whole new way.

Writing memoir is about truth telling and saying what's hard to say, yes, but I don't see it as a confessional booth where anything goes. It's not a pot of soup where you just throw anything in because you think it will spice it up. A memoir deserves the wisdom of discretion.

Talk about your terrible first drafts

When I write the first draft of a chapter, it's generally not very good. At least that's how I feel.

As a novice, I used to think it went like this: you sit down, you write it, if it isn't great, oh! you've failed. Back then when I wrote my terrible first drafts, I'd think, It's never going to get published, maybe I should dump the idea. Maybe I'm not that good of a writer.

My first sentence, my first paragraph, my first page, my first chapter cannot begin to match my expectations or the vision I have in my head. I had to learn to give myself permission to write badly at the outset. My strength, I discovered, was rewriting. I start with a raw draft, and I work and work and work. I'm notoriously slow and dogged and methodical about it.

It's a process, and it usually starts in this place where I think it's impossible. It'll never happen! I'm overwhelmed! But then slowly, slowly, it starts to emerge.

I love that moment. I can feel it in my body. This little dawning. The feeling always comes. Now I'm getting there, I think. But when I start a new book, or even a new chapter, I have no way of knowing that's going to happen. Each time I feel as if I've never done it before.

Sue Monk Kidd's Wisdom for Memoir Writers

- No matter how much you've written or published, hold on to the part of yourself that feels like a beginner. As the Zen saying goes: "In the beginner's mind there are many possibilities. In the expert's mind there are few."
- Read at the level you want to write.
- Discover your own truth, your own vision, your own voice. These things are your particular genius.
- Allow yourself to write badly at first; learn to be a consummate rewriter.
- Tell your truth, but do it with some discretion.
- Writing requires vast amounts of courage. In writing as in life, if you're going to err, it might as well be on the side of audacity.
- Writing is an amazing way to spend your life. It helps to be grateful for that, to stand in awe of it a little.

CHAPTER ELEVEN

Anne Lamott

It is all hopeless. Even for a crabby optimist like me, things couldn't be worse. Everywhere you turn, our lives and marriages and morale and government are falling to pieces. So many friends have broken children. The planet does not seem long for this world. Repent! Oh, wait, never mind. I meant: Help.

—Opening, *Help, Thanks, Wow,* 2012

⁓

It has been said that Sunday morning, church time, is the most segregated hour in America.

Here's another segregated hour: 7:30 p.m. at any book reading in America. Thanks to the balkanization of books into tinier and tinier categories and subcategories—literary versus commercial, fiction versus nonfiction, historical versus contemporary fiction, chick lit versus—what? ("dick lit"?); books for black versus white readers, left-wing versus right-, etc., etc.— authors' audiences tend to be as homogenous as most congregations.

Not so Anne Lamott's book events. They're as diverse as they are epic, and no wonder. Who doesn't love Anne Lamott? (One possible exception comes to mind: George W. Bush, whose sins she seems unable to forgive.) Lamott is the Dalai Lama of authors; a something-for-everyone writer, a unifying being in a divided, can't-we-just-get-along world. Under one curly roof, Anne Lamott encompasses a panoply of seemingly disparate traits, bringing fresh meaning to the phrase "defies categorization." She's a relentless activist and a self-deprecating comedian, a twelve-stepping, animal-loving, Christian grandmother whose wildly successful fiction and nonfiction books, essays, and speeches appeal to—well, just about everyone.

In 2003, Anne Lamott delivered the commencement speech at UC Berkeley. My son happened to be among the graduates, so I was among the parents who roared when she said, "I bet I'm beginning to make your parents really nervous. Here I am bragging about being a dropout, and unemployable, and making a pitch for you to follow your creative dreams, when what they want is for you to do well in your field, make them look good, and maybe also make a tiny fortune."

If you aren't yet a member of the Anne Lamott Fan Club, a promise and a warning: to read her is to love her.

THE VITALS

Birthday: April 10, 1954

Born and raised: San Francisco, California

Home now: Marin County, California

Family: Son Sam, 29; grandson Jax, 5

Schooling: Drew School; Goucher College

Day job: Nope

Notable notes:
- Before she published her first book, and before she got sober, Anne was a restaurant reviewer for now-defunct *California* magazine.
- Since its publication in 1994, Anne's *Bird by Bird* has been one of the world's top-selling writing books, with more than 1 million copies in print.
- In 1999, Academy Award–winning filmmaker Freida Lee Mock made a documentary about Anne Lamott, *Bird by Bird with Annie.*

Facebook: https://www.facebook.com/AnneLamott

Twitter: @annelamott

THE COLLECTED WORKS

Novels

Hard Laughter, 1980

Rosie, 1983

Joe Jones, 1985

All New People, 1989

Crooked Little Heart, 1997

Blue Shoe, 2002

Imperfect Birds, 2010

Grace (Eventually), 2007

Some Assembly Required, 2012

Help, Thanks, Wow, 2012

Stitches, 2013

Small Victories, 2014

Nonfiction

Operating Instructions, 1993

Bird by Bird, 1994

Traveling Mercies, 1999

Plan B, 2005

Essays, Columns (Partial Listing)

Salon.com

The New York Times Opinionator

Oprah.com

Sunset

Anne Lamott

Why I write about myself

God, I love writing memoirs. I love it so much more than writing novels.

Some people think novel writing is recreational. I don't really enjoy it. The sustained three years or so it takes to write a novel are so stressful. For me to write fiction, there has to be something deep inside me that's in there knitting itself, getting itself organized—a really deep arrival of something unavoidable. A novel will be a deep archeological work. That's what it takes to get to the truth and the depth of so many different characters—to establish relationships with them so they'll trust me enough to share with me what they're going through, what they would have done, instead of what I would rather that they do. When a novel rears its ugly head, I always sigh and think, Oh, shoot, I guess I'll be writing a novel. Then I think about how mentally ill I'm going to be for the entire time. My plan is not to write any more novels.

Writing a memoir is a lot more welcoming project. It's like going to the beach or the library. When I think about writing a memoir, I sometimes actually feel excited. First I think, I'd love to read that book. Second, I know it's doable.

Unlike novels, before you even sit down to write your memoir, it has a beginning, a middle, and an end. Something happened, and you write about it. I always used to tell my students to write the book they'd like to come upon, and I love to read memoirs, so they're the perfect thing for me to write.

Memoirist as missionary

I write memoirs because I have a passionate desire to be of even the tiniest bit of help. I like to write about the process of healing, of developing, of growing up, of becoming who we were born to be instead of who we always agreed to be.

It's sort of a missionary thing, to describe one person's interior, and to say we're probably raised not to think this or say it, but actually all of us feel it and have gone through it, and we all struggle with it. I feel like it's a gift I have to offer to people, to say, "This is what it's like for me, who you seem to like or trust. We're all like this. We're all ruined. We're all loved. We all feel like victims, we all feel better than."

There's no shame in that. Anybody you'd ever want to be friends with has had a tremendous amount of wounding in their past. If someone had an ideal childhood, and their parents really loved each other, and they were early proponents of equality, and their parents got lots and lots of therapy before they had kids, it's very unlikely that I'd want to sit with them for a cup of tea, let alone a meal. But if someone had very crazy parents and a lot of fear and tiptoeing around and whatnot, it's like, "Good, come have a seat."

Warning: memoir writing can be habit-forming

In 1993, after *Operating Instructions* came out, my publisher really wanted me to write a novel, for reasons that were strategic to my career. I begged my publisher to let me write *Bird by Bird* instead. I wrote it in six or seven months.

I'd been teaching writing at (Marin County's indie bookstore) Book Passage and giving lectures about writing for so long. I felt that so, so much of what people at workshops are taught is just b.s. It's so focused on publication, as if that's something that makes people happy, as if that's a reason for us all to be writing. I would have loved it if, when I was twenty, someone had written what I wrote in *Operating Instructions*. I felt a real imperative to write that kind of book on writing.

How a memoir becomes a book

Writing *Operating Instructions* was very casual. I just jotted down a few lines about Sam's babyhood every day. The fact that it became a book, let alone a book that people actually read, is still kind of shocking to me.

Then in 1997, I started writing personal columns for Salon .com. Some of them were really good. Some were the kind of stuff you have to write on deadline. Writing them was so liberating. The format I love the most is the 2,000- to 2,500-word complete beginning, middle, end story, about something that's either excruciating or seems to be.

Once I started to see that I could write these pieces that would organize themselves around one particular theme, I started working with the idea of a quilted memoir made up of those pieces.

Some Assembly Required was my publisher's idea. They wanted it because *Operating Instructions* had done so well. The idea seemed really obvious: all of a sudden I had a nineteen-year-old with a new baby.

I was glad to do it. I so believe in and love taking one area of my life and just telling that part of it, instead of having to figure out a long, sustained, book-length story. At first I was worried that the book would be really exploitive. But then my editor said, "It won't be exploitive if you don't exploit anyone."

And Sam was into doing it. He told me that *Operating Instructions* was the most important gift he'd ever had, the most important thing that ever happened to him. He wanted to give that gift to his son, Jax. He was much more into doing it than I was.

Sam was flailing in the world at that point. I didn't know if he'd be able to sustain the energy and attention it would take to do his part. But then he kept coming up with these pieces that I just loved loved loved.

Sometimes a book comes naturally

In 2009 I was on tour and my publisher heard me say, "Help, thanks, and wow" are the only prayers you need. They're the three-prayer equivalent of *Bird by Bird*."

He called me up and said, "I'd love a cup of that." That's how *Help, Thanks, Wow* came about.

Same as with *Bird by Bird*, I'd been talking about that stuff for oo long, I knew the book would come really naturally. And it did. It just came to me.

Sometimes a book just has to be written

When the Newtown shootings happened, I was stunned in a way that was even worse than the way I felt after 9/11. *Stitches* was a direct result of that.

I had a Sunday school class to teach right after the shootings, and I thought, What can I tell these children that's true? Then I remembered Barry Lopez's line, "All we have is compassion and stories," and I was off and running, writing about grief and coming through and how a community can somehow, somehow, somehow help us stand when we're knocked down at a life-threatening level, and the blessing of being part of that community and the blessing of receiving that love and solidarity and compassion and devotion.

When I read a book I want it to be written by somebody I trust who has a take on life that I trust. My hope with *Stitches* was to put together something in the face of Newtown that you could turn to as something sort of true. True, and maybe even helpful.

It looks easy. But it isn't

People think my memoirs are very easy to write because I do sound like I talk. They don't know it takes me five drafts for it to sound that way. But more than fifteen books later, I still struggle with the same feelings of self-worth, the same fear of failure, the same fears that I won't be able to pull it off, that the well is running dry.

It's not like I write a 2,500-word story and it comes out good or cohesive or sounding natural. It comes out herky-jerky and way, way too long and overwrought and it just sucks. The second draft is 30 percent better, but it's still terrible.

It's good not to hurt people

When I wrote my first couple of memoirs, I worried that I'd hurt people's feelings or make the people I love feel invaded. I don't worry about that anymore.

I know I'm not going to publish anything that anyone I'm close to would be hurt by or would hate. And I know how much I'll end up taking out. Telling the truth in memoir isn't telling *all* the truths. It's not spewing. Anything I'm writing will be completely crafted and edited before it's published.

I run everything I'm writing past everybody I'm writing about. I have a really clear sense of what's a boundary violation and what's not. I won't write intimate stuff about my son or my brothers or my closest friends. I'd never betray anyone's trust in a memoir. It's not worth it to me.

It's not always possible not to hurt people

In *Grace (Eventually)*, I wrote a piece about a friend. It was 100 percent affirming. It was a puff piece. She didn't want me to publish it. So I changed her name and my description of her life and her physical nature. I made all the details about her the opposite of what was true: her family, marriage, kids, dogs, career, everything. I was interested in the story, not the details. Nothing I changed was significant to the story. There was a 0 percent chance that anyone anywhere, even in her closest circle, would know it was her. And she went crazy. There were family secrets that I didn't tell, but even not telling them was too close for comfort.

She called me and said, "Let me put it this way: you won't

publish this." I said, "Let me put it this way: I will. You won't tell me what I will publish and what I won't."

Our friendship ended. I was severely attacked by her grown children, who were threatening litigation. Actually, her response to my story was a much better story than the one I published about her.

She wrote me last week and said, "We're friends for life. I've completely healed." I wanted to say, "You know what? I haven't. I could never trust you again because your response was so bizarre and so savage."

Sometimes Mom gets hurt

I wrote a piece about my mom in *Traveling Mercies*, and it really hurt her feelings. I thought it would be such a great thing to tell the truth about my mom, because my whole life had been about this made-up relationship, pretending I wasn't mad about the damage she'd done to me.

I wrote this very tender piece about her in her last days, when she had Alzheimer's. It wasn't even a critical piece. It just said that she could drive me crazy. Sadly she didn't have bad enough Alzheimer's. She read it and went bonkers. My mom's twin sister called me up and said, "You will never be forgiven for this, Annie."

The crisis passed. Then it turned out it was great to have told the truth about how deeply crazily I loved her *and* that she'd been a handful.

With memoirs, you break the contract you signed when you were three years old, promising not to ever, ever tell the truth, promising your family secrets would go with you to the grave.

In a family, that's life threatening. They tell you that if you ever tell the truth about the family, the long bony hand will come out of the sky and kill you.

You never know how people are going to react to a memoir

My older brother had been missing from our lives for a very long time. He sort of forgot to be there for my parents when they both had mortal brain diseases. My younger brother and I took care of them till the bitter end. John couldn't and didn't. But he was the one they loved the most: the first, the man.

A couple of years ago John decided to come back into our family, and I wrote a piece for my new book about what that was like. John was the first person I showed it to. I was sick with anxiety that it would be painful for him, or that he'd say, "Please don't use this." Instead, he wrote me, "You didn't tell me this would make me cry."

To be able to write that piece was such a gift. That's one of the possibilities of memoir: to give a gift to somebody. *Operating Instructions* was a gift to my best friend Pammy, much more than it was a gift to Sam. The gift of the memoir is getting to say on paper what most families never get to say in conversation.

Navel-gazer?

When I was working on my first couple of memoirs, I was worried that people would think I was navel-gazing or beating a dead horse. I talk about the same themes over and over and over again—family, and a little bit of healing here and there, and how horrible wounds are healed, and how we don't give up, and just how excruciating life is for some people a lot of the time, and how unfair and bizarre it is to even be here on earth.

But even if I wrote about the exact same events and experiences over and over, which I don't, what I wrote as a thirty-five-year-old mother is very, very different from what I write as a sixty-year-old woman. I do believe Barry Lopez was right: we're just in it for the stories. So I don't worry about being a navel-gazer anymore.

Criticism hurts

What I do worry about, inordinately, is reviews. I wish I didn't, but I do. I don't have twenty pages written and I'm already thinking about how the New York literary world is going to respond. You can't write based on how your book will be received, or you're just doomed.

But the critics are so powerful. And review space is so limited now. It's hard to get space unless you're one of the five New York literati darlings. *Stitches* is my fifteenth book and it still didn't get many reviews.

You hear writers say they don't read reviews, that reviews don't affect them. I think they're lying. Every writer I know cares very deeply about reviews. Every writer I know is very hurt by the bad ones, and very confused and saddened by the lack of reviews. If you're being honest, you can't help but care what your peers think. If your relatives see a bad review, it's just mortifying.

It's so courageous to put your stuff out there, especially

memoir. For people to see that you got beaten up is humiliating. Bad reviews really hurt. You feel so exposed.

For me it's like my entire childhood is flashing before my eyes, that I'm being told that what I thought was a work of art—and my creativity and my extremely hard work—was laughable or not as good as my earlier work, not that they reviewed my earlier work. The very worst review anxiety I felt was when I did the book with Sam. I don't love having bad reviews or being ignored, but I'd *hate* for people to come after my son.

Publication hurts

People in MFA programs think publishing is the pinnacle of creative success and esteem. It's actually just the opposite. You have to go through it a few times before you realize how toxic, how sick, how crushing the whole thing can be even if a book does relatively well, let alone if it doesn't.

I hate publication. It makes me extremely anxious. I can be at my most fragile for quite a long time, during that long, long period of waiting to see how a book is going to do. It's an extremely painful part of the process.

I get this feeling of *grippage* in my stomach before a book comes out. The easiest way not to have it is not to publish a lot more. I'm just too old for book tours. I'm sure you could find lots of people, like Margaret Atwood, who are a little older and they thrive on it. I don't thrive on it. I'm wasted by it. I hate being away from my family and my life—my animals, my church. I hate flying. The airports have become a god-awful mess. To think about not doing that is wonderful.

I've published four books in four years. I feel kind of tired of being out in the public all the time. So right now I'm not positive I need to keep publishing books. Or maybe it's just been too much, and I need a few years off.

It feels weird to think about stopping publishing, because I'm old, but I'm not that old. I'm not retirement age—not that I actually have a job. But I do this for a living.

I've been writing these mini memoirs on Facebook. I completely love doing that. I love the populism and the fact that it's free. If I could make a living writing one thousand words on Facebook every two weeks, I would.

I love my readers

I was in Grand Rapids this weekend. It was ten hours from my house to the Grand Rapids airport. I had to get up at four thirty in the morning. The traveling was horrible, but then I loved it so much. I gave two big talks and they went really well, and I felt such a connection and flow with my readers, and I felt how lucky I am that I just show up and tell the truth about my life, and because I have a sense of humor about it, that seems to help people.

The reason to write memoir is to put something important out into the collective consciousness, to distill one human life as you've come to understand it. I've got this one life I'm trying to understand, and as long as I'm trying to understand it, I imagine I'll be writing memoirs.

Anne Lamott's Wisdom for Memoir Writers

- Don't wait for inspiration. Point your finger at your head and march yourself to your desk. It's a great dream to do something that connects us with antiquity and with last week's news. So don't be a big whiny baby. Woman up and write.

- Everything that's happened to you is all yours. Just write it. You can worry about the legal issues and the next bad holiday dinner later. Tell the story that's in you to tell.

- All writing is collaborative, including memoir. Ask lots of people to help you remember details—people who were there for the experiences you had, and people who had similar experiences. Sometimes only someone else can remember what the stairs behind the kitchen looked like.

Chapter Twelve

Sandra Tsing Loh

I have just gotten off the phone with my friend and magazine editor, Ben. We have been talking about refinancing . . . It helps me to recall . . . the staid, rational person I was not too long ago: which is to say before I, a forty-something suburban mother, became involved in a wild and ill-considered extramarital affair.

—Opening, *The Madwoman in the Volvo*, 2014

Sandra Tsing Loh is often described, by herself and others, as "manic." In her one-woman show *Mother on Fire*, she was downright maniacal. In it, Sandra paced the stage, gesticulating wildly, delivering a rapid-fire, obscenity-laden monologue on her life and everyone in it who dared to displease her.

"After we follow Loh on her journey—through fluorescent-lit schools, complicated female friendships, the elaborate dances of decades-old marriages," a *Salon* reviewer wrote of Sandra's 2008 memoir by the same name, "we emerge euphoric, flush with community spirit and able to laugh at our own insanity."

Emphasis on "able to laugh." In her one-woman shows, her memoirs, her NPR dispatches, and her personal essays for *The Atlantic* and other publications, Sandra Tsing Loh puts it all out there, holding up a mirror to the maniac in all of us, daring us to look away. And we can't, we can't. Because what she's holding up, really, is the good, the bad, the ugly truth.

The Vitals

Birthday: February 11, 1962

Born and raised: Malibu, California

Home now: Los Angeles, California

Family: Daughters Madeline, 14, and Susannah, 12

Schooling: Bused to Santa Monica High School; BS in physics from the California Institute of Technology; master's in professional writing from the University of Southern California

Current projects: Contributing editor, *The Atlantic*; commentator, KPCC; adjunct professor of visual art and science communication at the University of California, Irvine

Notable notes:

- During a 2004 episode of Sandra's KCRW show, *The Loh Life*, an engineer neglected to bleep the word "fuck" from her monologue; KCRW canceled her show (and she gained some national visibility) as a result.
- As a solo performer, Sandra wrote and performed a number of one-woman shows, including *Aliens in America* and *Bad Sex with Bud Kemp* (both off-Broadway at Second Stage Theatre) and *Mother on Fire*, which earned her a spot on *Variety*'s list of 50 most influential comedians.
- Sandra's *Atlantic* essay "The Bitch Is Back" was selected for inclusion in *The Best American Essays* in 2012, and her book on the same topic, *The Madwoman in the Volvo*, was named one of the *New York Times*' 100 Most Notable Books of 2014.

Facebook: https://facebook.com/MadwomanInTheVolvo

Twitter: @SandraTsingLoh

Website: members.authorsguild.net/sandratloh/

The Collected Works

Novel

If You Lived Here, You'd Be Home by Now, 1997

Memoirs

Depth Takes a Holiday, 1996

Aliens in America, 1997

A Year in Van Nuys, 2001

Mother on Fire, 2008

The Madwoman in the Volvo, 2014

Essays, Columns, Radio Appearances (Partial Listing)

The Atlantic

The New York Times

New York

Vogue

Elle

Harper's Bazaar

Saveur

NPR's *Morning Edition*

PRI's *Marketplace*

This American Life

KPCC's *The Loh Life*

The Loh Down on Science (syndicated)

Sandra Tsing Loh

Why I write about myself

Memoir is my genre. Everything I do comes out of that genre: the radio commentaries I've been doing weekly for sixteen years, my solo theater shows, my long-form magazine pieces, my books.

I didn't find memoir. Memoir found me. I started writing in my twenties. In the various writing workshops I was in, we were all trying to write the next great American novel—or at least the next great Tama Janowitz short story collection. I found that when I wrote stories in the first person, readers found them more energetic and interesting than when I wrote them in third.

My story "My Father's Chinese Wives" was the turning point for me. This was the true-life tale of my divorced Chinese father, in his seventies, deciding to marry what would become a series of, essentially, Chinese mail-order brides. First I wrote it from the point of view of someone I named something like Susan Chao. Everyone kept asking, "But isn't this your dad? Isn't this you?" Eventually I just rewrote it from my own point of view, and then performed it as a twenty-minute monologue at Highways, and a star was born. Unfortunately for me, what I didn't realize at the time was that the star was my dad.

In any case, that story grew into a show, *Aliens in America*, produced by Second Stage (off-Broadway). That was the launch-pad for everything that came after. I should note also that I am fortunate as a writer/performer to have come of age, if you will, during the great flowering of public radio. Every monologue in *Aliens in America* also ran as a piece on *This American Life*. Ira Glass made me!

Writing memoir is witnessing

Whenever I wrote a short story I'd be working out some problem or other in my mind, trying to find a meaning or narrative or context for something that had happened to me, something I was trying to understand. In my twenties, admittedly, it was bad dates. Not very fashionable literarily, but you have to write what you know, even if it's unpublishable.

It's just as much fun—sometimes more—to create other voices and other characters. But sometimes when I write memoir it's a kind of witnessing. When my oldest daughter became kindergarten aged, I was stunned by how traumatic the Los Angeles school search was, what a monster I was turning into, and at how unexplored this terrain was—the things that nice, Democrat mothers start candidly, truly thinking when contemplating sending their white kids to 97 percent Hispanic poor public schools. In this case, it was entirely appropriate to tell my own story. It was authentic, it assigned all the hypocrisy to me, rather than to others, and as a result, I think the book and show were both funnier and more persuasive because my character took the fall.

My menopause memoir came from an assignment I got from my editor Ben Schwarz, then at *The Atlantic*. I've always thought of *The Atlantic* as a very male magazine. But Ben believed that the experiences women go through—and what they think about them—are crucial indicators of larger forces in our culture.

Atlantic pieces are long—four thousand words—so the inspiration is different than it is for shorter work. It's like poetry, where you may ruminate and develop a lot of ideas but to get the opening and sustaining emotional pitch, drive, and obsession for the piece you have to wait for the heavens to open. It takes a while to wrap my arms around each one of these long-form essays.

My editor thought menopause was a significant phenomenon that hadn't been written about very vividly, even though today almost 50 percent of American women are currently menopausal. He thought it was the perfect kind of piece for me.

I was resistant. I didn't see what the story was. Then I entered my late forties and started having these mysterious severe depressions. Plus I was forgetful. I couldn't keep track of my own thoughts or have a sense of humor about any of it. People kept telling me I might be in perimenopause. At which point I told my editor, "You're right. Someone has to write a piece on menopause. But it can't be me because I'm too bloated, too depressed, too brain-dead to do it. Or anything else."

Sometimes writing your truth hurts you

The most painful thing for me to write about was when I had an affair and blew up my marriage. It was a terrifying, exhilarating, traumatic, amazing, horrific time.

I'd written about my life for so long, but I'd always been able to craft myself as a somewhat sympathetic character. My books were about me being a public school advocate, me being a suburban mom next door. No matter how self-deprecating I was, at the end I'd always come out on the side of the good, with a positive message, like "All children deserve a great education."

Then I wrote that very controversial thing to say as a mother: I was married with kids and I fell madly in love with someone and I destroyed two families and now I'm divorced. That wasn't exactly "America's sweetheart" material.

Nowadays, in the age of the Internet, every writer has to deal with the swiftness and intensity of reader comments. Readers go online and give their opinions—the good, the bad, and the extremely ugly. The comments were horrific. They said I was a sad, pathetic woman. They wondered why *The Atlantic* had given me space on the page. They canceled their subscriptions. I've never been afraid to write anything I needed to write. But that was a tough one. I had to tell my story and take my lumps.

When you're a memoirist you have to keep writing your story—however not-ready-for-prime-time it is. I'm not a mystery writer. My material is my life.

Sometimes writing your truth hurts others

My concern, when I wrote that story, was not so much how I'd come across, or whether I'd get attacked, but to try to protect the privacy of the other people involved. It's one's responsibility, if one can, to avoid implicating others. No one in your life chooses to be in your story.

I'd wrecked two marriages and two families. Everyone was, like, "You've already done enough damage. Now you're going to describe it in print?" It's the most complex thing about writing memoir: you can't avoid writing about real people with real feelings, and most of them aren't you.

I tried to write about my affair in a way that made it clear that I was the worst-behaved character, to cast blame on no one other than me. And I renamed and changed the identifying characteristics of all the other characters.

One thing that helped was that the straight men in my life don't necessarily read my material too closely. They have other things they're more interested in. They don't do line-by-line readings and interpretations the way females do. Even in good times, my husband wouldn't rush to read stuff I'd written. After twenty years he was used to my general chatter. Having our lives in print was like not-unpleasant white noise to him. A working artist himself, he respects people's professions, which is what my writing, in the end, is.

A little disclaimer goes a long way

In my work, there is always a disclaimer that says up front, This is not witnessing, not a documentary; it's a composite. Whatever you want to reveal about yourself is up to the writer. You have to shape your material. If you need a character to say a particular thing, invent a character and have him or her say that. If other people have secrets they don't want you to tell, you shouldn't tell them. You don't want someone who looks like a small sad puffy owl described that way. So just change his description. Make him skinny, seven feet tall, and lynx-like if you must.

I have an older brother and older sister. Until now, my brother (the "passive" middle child) has not come forth as a character. By contrast, my bossy sister has uttered such memorable lines I've had to give her a different name so I can't be sued. My two daughters appear under different names.

I've seen people write exactly what happened, exactly what the people looked like. You can call that memoir. Maybe the word "memoir" isn't useful in my case; perhaps "creative nonfiction" is more useful.

Je ne regrette rien

I'm not sorry about anything I've written, including what I wrote about my affair. So many people responded not just negatively but positively to it—people who have gone through a lot of pain also.

When you tell your story, other people start telling theirs. It gives everyone a bigger span of experience than just the ones they've had. When anybody tells a candid story of failure or sorrow, it tends to make the world bigger and safer for everyone. Not everything we experience is out of the good behavior playbook. Marriage, for example, is challenging. I salute anyone who tries to sustain it. Then there's menopause. Women don't like to talk about it. But since I wrote my menopause book, I get letters all the time, saying, "I felt so desolate and alone until I read your book. I laughed, I cried, I felt more normal."

My aspiration as a memoirist is to make the largest possible segment of humanity feel that I've addressed part of their story. It's all about the audience. I want my readers to feel that I've told my story well, that I've given them some solace. Whatever I've been through, I want to make it better for someone else.

You might think you know me. You would be wrong

On paper I sound really manic and crazy. But in real life, I have to hold a lot of people in my family together. I have to be solid and reliable, at least with my daughters. My persona on the page is much quirkier than I am in real life.

I'm a professional writer. That's what I do. If editors would assign me books that weren't about me, I'd be happy to write them. My next book is me again: funny essays on midlife. The journey continues, next installation. I've written journalism also, and still do, and enjoy it, but my editors tend to want my voice mixed in. I am a sort of Costco-priced Virgil to the noisome bolgias of modern life.

My agent says, "You have to think about how to make every book a bit different. It's a challenge to make it fresh." In the end I'm the queen of a shoe box. Writing on the page is what I do. It may pay a lot, it may pay a little, it doesn't matter. Way back in my youth I had an offer to write a TV pilot for $25,000. It was a huge amount of money at that time, but I couldn't see writing it the way they wanted me to, so I quit. The next day I got my first NPR *Morning Edition* commentary accepted. The fee was $50. I said, "Okay, I'll eat beans."

To my detriment, I'm a person who cannot fake my way through meetings. That's why I don't have a million-dollar home in the Hollywood Hills. It's sad for my children's college tuitions, but when it comes to crafting a piece of writing, I'm just not a team player, damn it.

Sandra Tsing Loh's Wisdom for Memoir Writers

- You can't do it alone. Get a good writing workshop or join a writing group. Meet with them at least twice a month for two hours. That's your tribe, the ones who will be with you and hold you accountable. They'll make sure you show up every two weeks with pages. They can be two pages, they can be terrible pages, they can be your Trader Joe's grocery list—but they'll be your pages.

- It's really important to read, and widely. Writing a memoir is not just putting your experience into a format. It has to be entertaining and compelling. You have to be able to name the top three memoirs you loved, and you have to try to write yours in that style.

- Don't rely on Facebook for getting an awesome, legendary writer (Cheryl Strayed! Cheryl Strayed!) to read your three-hundred-page manuscript just because you are her fan. Instead, build genuine connections with the people—writers or not—around you. If you ask a favor of others, be sure to offer a favor back. By nurturing real connections, you will become more experienced, more powerful, and more closely knit as a tribe.

CHAPTER THIRTEEN

James McBride

I'm dead.

You want to talk about my family and here I been dead to them for fifty years. Leave me alone. Don't bother me. They want no parts of me and me I don't want no parts of them. Hurry up and get this interview over with. I want to watch Dallas.

—Opening, *The Color of Water*, 1996

~~~

Spoiler alert: if you're a sensate being, and you go to James McBride's website, it's likely to widen your eyes, tickle your ears, spread a grin across your face, and tell you much of what you need to know about the man who sits on a stoop on his home page alternately typing and playing the sax.

In case you need details, the bio page offers this. "In addition to being a musician, James has other talents. He's the worst dancer in the history of African Americans, bar none, going back to slave time and beyond. He should be legally barred from dancing at any party he attends. He dances with one finger in the air like a white guy."

Okay, so: funny guy. Bad dancer. Also, musician who studied at the Oberlin Conservatory and has written music and lyrics for Anita Baker, Grover Washington, Jr., and PBS's Barney.

Also, screenwriter who cowrote and coproduced *Red Hook Summer* with Spike Lee, among other film projects.

Oh, and also, bestselling author of three novels and one blockbuster memoir. He earned his master's degree in journalism at Columbia University at age twenty-two, was a staff writer for publications including the *Boston Globe* and *People* magazine, and won a National Book Award for his 2013 novel *The Good Lord Bird*. His first book, *The Color of Water,* has sold more than 2.5 million copies in sixteen languages and is required reading in schools across the country.

If there's one theme that emerges from all the interviews with all the memoirists in this book, it's this: "Memoirs should matter." Not just to the memoirist and the people who are flattered and incensed about their portrayals in his or her books, but to the state of the world in which their readers live. *The Color of Water* matters. James McBride matters.

THE VITALS

Birthday: September 11, 1957

Born and raised: New York, New York

Home now: New York and Lambertville, New Jersey

Family: Three children: Jordan, Azure, Nash

Schooling: BA, Oberlin College; Oberlin Conservatory of Music; master's in journalism, Columbia University; Distinguished Writer in Residence, New York University

Day job: Nope

Notable notes:
- Like his eleven siblings, James McBride is a product of the New York public schools.
- At the age of thirty, James quit his job as a features writer for the *Washington Post* to pursue a career in music.
- James's April 2007 *National Geographic* story, "Hip Hop Planet," is considered a landmark treatise on African American music and culture.

Facebook: https://www.facebook.com/pages/James-McBride/109446129081488

Website: www.jamesmcbride.com

THE COLLECTED WORKS

Novels

Miracle at St. Anna, 2002

Song Yet Sung, 2008

The Good Lord Bird, 2013

Memoir

The Color of Water, 1996

Essays, Columns, Articles (Partial Listing)

Essence

Rolling Stone

The New York Times

James McBride

Why I write about myself

Before *The Color of Water* came out, I did a lot of stuff that failed. I worked in musical theater and I failed in that. If you put my musical theater résumé together, I would look like a pretty promising composer, but it wasn't like Stephen Sondheim was spinning around in bed at night worrying about me. Neither was Wynton Marsalis. Or Tom Wolfe or Kurt Vonnegut.

I didn't know what a memoir was when I wrote *Water*. I didn't pay any attention to the label of memoir versus nonfiction versus fiction. I just thought it was a good story and I had to tell it.

I don't really care what anyone else does. I don't follow the careers of other writers. I work with blinders on. I know what I have to do. The book I wrote as a memoir might be the kind of thing another writer would write as fiction.

Water started with a magazine piece I wrote for the *Globe* back in the early eighties. I was talking to an editor there, and somehow or other the subject of my mother came up. I mentioned that I was pretty sure she was Jewish, and he said, "You should follow up on that." So I did, and I found out that she was; and I wrote about what I learned, and it was published in the *Globe* and the *Philadelphia Inquirer* on Mother's Day.

After that I started writing a book based on the magazine piece. I worked on it a little at a time. I went to Africa. I did my work for the *Globe*. I worked on the book when I could. The finished book might feel like the writing of it was immediate, but it wasn't. It happened over time, in bursts, and most of the time I spent on it was research.

The older I got, the more I began to appreciate who my mother was. I did the work because I started to see that my mother was very interesting. It was kind of an evolutionary process that happened as I was maturing into my late twenties, early thirties. I was starting to see the world a little more clearly.

I started to see that in the world at large, the stuff we hadn't considered very important was actually incredibly important: race, religion, money, power.

But I didn't have any specific aspirations when I wrote *Water*. I just wanted to get the rest of the advance. I don't really find my musings to be strong enough to justify my writing a memoir. I don't have that kind of patience. I just don't think I'm that interesting.

Lean times, lean book

Water came out in 1996. At the time I was a full-time musician, traveling a lot, playing a lot of crummy clubs, eating bad food. I was struggling, really. And the leanness of that life probably had an impact on that work in the sense that I wanted it to be done, and I didn't want to be driven by the kind of angst that was kicking me around in those years.

The narrative of the book was as thin and as muscled as my life was at that time. You know, with every story you do, you're trying to shove a lot of things into the keyhole and drag the reader with you. You have to narrow the focus of the story so it has the push of a creek in a narrow spot.

Struggling is good for writing

My life is still a struggle—just a different kind.

A year ago I started a music program in the church my mother and father founded in the same housing project where I was born. It's a lot of work. If I could retire and do nothing else I'd probably just do that. It means so much to me to do it.

There's a lot of struggle involved in getting these kids into church and into this music program.

I think that kind of struggle is important for a writer. I think it's a mistake for a writer to sit around coffee shops musing about bullshit. I think it's a waste of time and I never do it.

The people I work with in the church don't know I'm a National Book Award winner. They don't know about *The Color of Water*. Most of them haven't read any of my books. Many of the older ones knew my mother, or knew of her. We're connected in that way.

I don't like sitting around talking about work. Invariably it ends up with, "I didn't like this book for that reason; I didn't like this one for that reason." A writer can't be too negative. You have to have a little bit of innocence to be a good writer. Whatever you have to do to preserve that innocence—the "is that so?" element—you should do it. You can't be someone who knows everything—"been there, done that." If you know everything you shouldn't be a writer. You should be God.

You need that sense of discovery as a writer, and part of that comes from the attitude you have. You have to stay away from people and places that foster cynicism and bitterness.

If I work hard at anything, it's that. I still take the bus. I still move around in circumstances where people don't know who I am. Because I ain't nobody, really. I'm still the same person. When I started writing, I didn't really know what writers did. I thought they sat around drinking coffee and sleeping with one another, then writing about it. I'm more of a writer now than I was then, but I'm still not one of those kinds of people. I don't go to writers' conventions or do big writer talks.

Ready, aim, don't fire

When you're writing a memoir, you have to be careful because you don't want to bruise people too much. You have to give people the benefit of the doubt.

It's really not beneficial on the page or through a blog or through any sort of written public word to blast people, unless they are truly deserving. A scamming lawyer or politician—yeah, you can aim your bazooka on them directly, and drop the hammer on them, and sleep tight.

But most of us don't deserve that kind of treatment. If someone's a racist or a sexist or a homophobic idiot, you have to kind of leave them to God. Just show them as they are, but don't blast away. Because everyone is capable of change.

Writing a memoir, you have to keep that in mind. You can't use a book as a kind of "I'm going to get back at them" exercise. You're not writing it for that reason. You write a memoir for the same reason you write a song—to help someone feel better. You don't write it to show how small you are or how dumb they are. You're trying to share from a sense of humbleness. It's almost like you're asking forgiveness of the reader for being so kind as to allow you to indulge yourself at their expense.

When I was writing *Water* I was very careful to respect my mother's family. I was very cognizant that most of those people didn't know me or any of my siblings. I didn't want to tommy-gun them. They had no choice about what happened. My mother did something that wasn't that cool, given where she came from. She broke free from the constraints of her life. I was raised to believe that everyone is different. The things that work for you may not work for other people. So I was careful to change their names to protect their privacy.

I kept my siblings out of the book as much as I could. With regards to my own privacy, I didn't dramatize it or soft-pedal it. I played it straight. I didn't really like divulging some of my activities as a high school kid. I'm ashamed of that stuff. I was not real pleased about putting it on the page, but I did it. And I did it without mentioning my friends who were involved.

Postracial publishing? Not so much

Publishers love the idea of a black person who's showing they were a thug doing dope and crack—the whole business of "I was lost but now I'm found; I was blind but now I see." This is a real problem for black writers. The industry is accustomed to black writers writing about pain and struggle. I can think of a half-dozen white writers who write about the same things and never had to deal with being marginalized. They're just seen as writers, period.

There's very little room in the publishing industry for minority writers. I don't know if that's anyone's fault. The industry tries to address the problem, but essentially it's a personal one. Each of us has to do what we can personally do to inch things forward just a little bit.

Another problem for black writers is that black people simply don't read enough. If you say that, people get insulted, but it's true. I have tons of black readers now, but when *Water* came out, most people who came to the early readings were white women and white Jewish women, and I was thankful they showed up.

I happen to think that a good black writer is the one who writes a book anyone will like. If a writer's good, readers will read those books and feel illuminated. That's the only way our industry will continue to grow. We have to embrace writers who are different just like we embrace a president who's different. If we don't, as a society we'll wither on the vine.

I wouldn't say it's getting better for writers of color. There are better and better writers of color, but they're not getting a shot. A lot of really good Asian American writers are starting to publish, like Chang-rae Lee, but I have yet to see a plethora of books by Americans of other hues.

It's not just a function of prejudice. The publishing industry is under so much pressure. A writer gets a book deal, and the book gets trotted out for six weeks, and if it doesn't sell, it's gone. So many young writers go through that. They don't have a shot at a second or third book. That's a real problem that's industry-wide for all writers.

To make our industry relevant we need really good editors who aren't looking for the next Hemingway, but for the next Tupac Shakur.

It's bigger than a publishing problem. We have a great black president, but what would happen if we had a great black vice president? A great black Speaker of the House? Why is it okay to have one black neighbor, but when ten black families move in, the neighborhood changes and stores close down—the kinds of problems that Detroit has right now?

Compared to the problems most people have, these are good problems. I don't want to bellyache about them.

Blah, blah, blog

In this world of blogging and telecommuting and Twitter, memoirists have to speak to deeper things.

We're writing memoirs 140 characters at a time, which means we're basically writing nothing. If you're writing nothing maybe you're living nothing. Before you put your story down, first change the manner in which you're living. If you do that, you won't find yourself writing a Broadway show with five minutes of spiritual uplift and then everyone goes home.

If you walk around with earplugs in, that won't give you something to say. Nothing you're going to write will be of import. Put those earbuds away and join the Peace Corps in Peru. That'll give you something to work with.

James McBride's Wisdom for Memoir Writers

- If I were an aspiring memoirist, the first thing I'd do is go visit my grandparents for a couple of months. Drop everything and stay with them. Cook their food. Deliver their groceries. Go to bingo night with them. Let them pull you backwards into their lives. Whatever they have to say is a bankbook for you as a memoirist. You'll see yourself in everything they do, even if they drive you nuts.

- Know that the writing will lead you into places you can't imagine you'll go. In my experience, writing comes from a place beneath intellectual consciousness. The only way to get to that place is by writing. Trust the magic of that process.

- Be wildly ambitious about your writing, and forget the stuff connected to writing. To use a sports metaphor: keep your eye on the ball. Publishing is not the ball. Getting an agent is not the ball. Winning the National Book Award is not the ball. The writing is the ball.

- Spend a lot of time figuring out what your story wants to say. Then figure out who the central characters are that you need to visit. Then report the hell out of it. You have to research your own life. Go back to the old 'hood; walk by your old house. You count the rooms, you eat the food, you drink the coffee, you sit in the bar, you go to the gas station and ask for directions. You have to breathe the air. Nothing might come of any of it, but you can't train just one muscle. You have to train the whole body.

CHAPTER FOURTEEN

Dani Shapiro

*I grew up the only child of older parents. If I were to give you
a list of all the facts of my early life that made me a writer,
this one would be near the top.* Only child. Older parents.
It now almost seems like a job requirement.

—Opening, *Still Writing*, 2013

Mention Dani Shapiro to any writer, editor, agent, or
reader who's had even a few moments in her presence,
and you're likely to be met with a faceful of smile, followed by a
stream of laudatory adjectives. "Brilliant." "Generous." "Humble." "Brave." "Self-aware." "Kind." And, of course, the blindingly obvious "gorgeous."

Raised by Orthodox Jews, Dani Shapiro has wrestled with
religion and spirituality, the subject of her bestselling 2010
memoir, *Devotion*, since childhood—internally, and on the
page. "I could no more reject my Judaism," Dani told an interviewer, "than reject being female, or being a mother, or a wife,
or a writer, or any of the things that most define me."

The depth of Dani Shapiro's oeuvre reflects the range of her
passions and curiosities. *Playing with Fire*, her first novel, was published in 1990, followed by two more novels in rapid succession,

and then a memoir, and then two more novels, and then a memoir, and then her most recent, a soulful how-to on the craft and practice of writing. Between books Dani writes reviews, essays, and travel stories for *The New Yorker*, *The New York Times Book Review*, *O, The Oprah Magazine*, *Vogue*, and *Elle*, among many others. What pervades and unifies her writings and her life is a thoughtful inquiry into the human condition, at once grounded and ethereal.

In 2013, two decades into her publishing career, Dani's agent uttered the two-word benediction every writer longs to hear—"Oprah called." For her appearance on Oprah's *Super Soul Sunday*, Dani prepared by intensifying her yoga and meditation practice so that she'd be centered for the experience. "It was surreal with all those lights and cameras," she said after the fact. "One of the producers said, 'Just be yourself,' and I thought, 'Being yourself is hard, hard work.'"

Luckily for her readers, Dani Shapiro does that work—and makes it look easy.

THE VITALS

Birthday: April 10, 1962

Born and raised: New York, New York

Home now: Litchfield County, Connecticut

Love life: Married to filmmaker Michael Maren

Kids: Jacob, 15

Schooling: Studied with Grace Paley at Sarah Lawrence College

Day job: Contributing editor, *Condé Nast Traveler*; leader of writing workshops nationally and internationally

Notable notes:
- Shortly after 9/11, Dani, Michael, and Jacob moved out of New York City, anticipating a quieter life. Instead, her new friends and neighbors in Connecticut included Arthur Miller, William Styron, Frank McCourt, Mia Farrow, and Milos Forman.
- In 1999 Dani adapted Oscar Wilde's story "The Happy Prince" for HBO; in 2000 she cowrote a screenplay based on her first memoir, *Slow Motion*, with her husband, Michael.
- Son Jacob's bar mitzvah, which Dani calls "the happiest day of my life," was officiated by two lesbian rabbis. Dani played piano; Jacob played ukulele.

Facebook: https://www.facebook.com/danijshapiro

Instagram: daniwriter

Twitter: @danijshapiro

Website: www.danishapiro.com

THE COLLECTED WORKS

Novels

Playing with Fire, 1990

Fugitive Blue, 1992

Picturing the Wreck, 1995

Family History, 2003

Black & White, 2007

Memoirs

Slow Motion, 1998

Devotion, 2010

Still Writing, 2013

Articles and Short Stories

The New Yorker

The New York Times Book Review

Elle

Vogue

Tin House

Electric Literature

Dani Shapiro

Why I write about myself

Writing memoir started for me by accident, as did much of my writing life and everything good in it.

By 1997 I'd written three novels, and I became aware that there was something haunting me that ran through all of them. In each book, something came out of the blue—some sudden catastrophe—and overtook the protagonist. To whatever extent we're ever in control when we write fiction, I knew that this was something I wasn't in control of. I wasn't walking the dog; the dog was walking me.

I had this instinct that I needed to stop fictionalizing the story that was haunting me: my parents' car accident, my father's death, my mother's broken bones, the way my entire family changed in an instant. Telling the story in my novels, I hadn't remotely accomplished what I'd hoped. The only way to do that was to write it as a memoir.

I'm not a believer in memoir as catharsis. It's a misapprehension that readers have that by writing memoir you're purging yourself of your demons. Writing memoir has the opposite effect. It embeds your story deep inside you. It mediates the relationship between the present and the past by freezing a moment in time.

Truth in memoir is a lie

The idea of truth in memoir is absurd. Memory is utterly mutable, changeable, and constantly in motion. You can't fact-check memory.

If I'd written my first memoir twenty or thirty years later, it would have been an entirely different book. The relationship between my self and my story would have changed. I'd be at a different point in my life, informed by different life experiences.

Here's a case in point. While I was working on *Devotion* in 2009, I found myself rewriting a scene I'd described a decade earlier in *Slow Motion*. There was a copy of *Slow Motion* three feet from my desk, but I decided not to read the scene the way I'd written it the first time. I wrote it as I remembered it in 2009.

When I compared the two versions, every detail was identical, except one. In both, it's a crystal clear, freezing February day in 1986. I'm in a hospital corridor, moments after my father died. I'm wearing a tight black skirt and a gold silk blouse and high-heeled boots. In *Slow Motion*, my sister bursts in and says, "Why aren't you with Dad? How could you have left his room?" I realize that I've betrayed my father; it's a tenet of Orthodox Judaism to never leave a body alone.

In *Devotion*, the same thing happens—except it's my uncle, not my sister, who's furious at me for leaving my father alone. I'm wearing the same outfit, the weather is the same, the same words are said, I have the same emotional response, but those words are coming out of the mouths of two different people. I didn't even think for one second of aligning the scenes so the two memoirs would be in sync. That would have been cheating, and not the point of memoir at all. Besides, it also struck me as a great teaching story.

When *Devotion* came out, my friend the great Buddhist teacher Sylvia Boorstein told me, "You've written a book about what you know now." The idea being, that's all we can do. We'll know more later. That's always true for a writer, but it's truest of memoir. Sometimes I think the perfect life's work for a memoirist might be to write the same book every ten years.

I don't write about me. I write about that girl

Whenever I publish a memoir, people ask me how I can stand to feel so exposed. But when I'm writing, I don't feel that I'm remotely exposing myself. When I wrote my first memoir, *Slow Motion*, I came to think of my younger self as "that girl." Or sometimes even, "oh, that poor girl."

Vivian Gornick refers to this phenomenon as a surrogate persona. It's not a trick. Particularly in writing *Slow Motion*, I had a willingness to reveal some unattractive, difficult, unethical, complex aspects of my own behavior. It was part of my history that I was trying to excavate and take and shape. But I didn't feel I was exposing myself; rather, I was creating that persona, that character.

One of the greatest gifts of writing memoir is having a way to shape that chaos, looking at all the pieces side by side so they make more sense. It's a supreme act of control to understand a life as a story that resonates with others. It's not a diary. It's taking this chaos and making a story out of it, attempting to make art out of it. When you're a writer, what else is there to do?

How I know it's a memoir

I've never had a piece of fiction announce itself as what it wants to be. A few short stories morphed into longer pieces, but those were more like tryouts for novels than stories. Every piece I've ever written announces itself as what it wants to be, whether fiction or memoir. I've occasionally had a short story grow into a novel, but otherwise—whether essay, story, memoir, novel, or screenplay—the thing knows what it wants to be, the form it wants to take.

But when it comes to the work itself, novels are shyer, slower to come into focus. Fiction requires a tremendous amount of patience. A single image or a piece of language might stick around a long time before everything else fills in around it.

It's different with memoir. When I'm embarking on a memoir it's crystal clear. It's a very different feeling. Memoir is much more assertive. Memoir comes up and bangs me on the head and says, "This is what you're doing." There's a lot I don't know when I begin—the way in, the structure. All of that isn't necessarily clear, but the fact of it is. The writer sitting at her desk knows whether she's in the territory of imagination or in the territory of memory.

Memoirists have to cull and pick and choose and be very discerning about what we put in and leave out of our stories. There should be a sign above the desk of every memoirist that reads, "Everything doesn't belong."

One of my favorite quotes about writing is what Aristotle wrote, in *Poetics*: "Action is not plot, but merely the result of pathos." If you have characters, you have pathos. If you have pathos, you have action. That's plot.

In memoir you've already had the pathos, the action, the

plot. The question is which story you'll tell, which window you'll look through. What's the frame around that story? What's the art in the telling? What's the discovery? I know what happened, so now what? What's interesting about this? What's a narrative that's interesting to read, to write? You're putting pieces together to see what kind of music they make. It's like stitching together a quilt, creating order that isn't chronological order—it's emotional, psychological order.

Writing well is the best revenge

Revenge is a really terrible reason to write a memoir. One, it doesn't feel good ultimately. Two, it doesn't make for a good book. Revenge on the page reeks. A writer with an agenda is no longer trustworthy. She becomes an unreliable narrator of her own life.

Students have asked me how a writer knows if she's writing out of revenge. Here's a clue: she thinks to herself, "I can't wait for so-and-so to read this."

Most memoirists' impetus comes from a profound need to understand and be understood. The crafting, the culling of a story is an act of control. You're saying, "Understand this about me, about my family, my history, my story."

Kurt Vonnegut once said that every writer writes for an audience of one. That audience changed for me with each memoir. With *Devotion*, I had the feeling that someday my son might read that book and be able to understand his mother and a time in our lives from my point of view. I imagined that after I was gone, the book might be meaningful to him.

With *Slow Motion*, my father was my audience of one, even

though he had been dead for quite a few years. I was trying to get our relationship right on the page. I have a working philosophy that's deepened over the years that we have no control over what happens to us, but we do have control over what we do with it, how it deepens us or doesn't deepen us. All my writing life, memoir has been an ongoing attempt to look at my relationships with both of my parents again and again through the lens of the passage of time.

Memoir gives you special things to worry about

When I was writing *Slow Motion*, I was very conscious of not wanting to hurt my mother. I didn't care about my ex-boyfriend. My father was dead. I had other relatives in the book, but they didn't come off in a negative way. If I could have sent my mother on an around-the-world cruise and had her come back when the book had passed from public consciousness, I would have done it.

As I was writing *Slow Motion*, I had to play tricks on myself to keep going. First, I told myself that I didn't have to publish it. It was completely unrealistic, of course; I had a contract, and I'd already spent the money. But telling myself I could change my mind gave me freedom to write without self-censorship.

When I finished the first draft, I asked a friend who had a teenage daughter to give it a "mother read"—to look for potshots, anything that felt unnecessary and hurtful. My friend came back with a couple of phrases and sentences and I took them out. They weren't necessary to the arc of the book or the characterization of my relationship with my mother.

I waited until the book was in galleys to give it to my mother. Here's what I learned: it was useless to have worried about what would upset her. She was angry about tiny details in the book that I hadn't even considered, and yet the things I did think would upset her sailed right by. The moral of the story was, We can't know what is going to impact another person, or why.

After I gave my mother the galleys, her therapist called and asked me to meet with her. What can I say? We were all New York Jews. I gave the therapist a set of galleys so she could read it before my mother did. After she read it, she said she didn't think there was anything that would upset my mother, that it was very fair to her. I had two thoughts. First, that this therapist didn't know my mother at all, and second, that my mother had been wasting her money for years.

Ultimately, though it took a long time to really sink in, my mother was devastated by the memoir. She was a very difficult person, and when people in her life heard that her daughter had written a memoir, they all read it as a way of trying to understand her: her doorman, her lawyer, her dentist, her neighbors. I couldn't have imagined such a thing happening. It was like she was in *The Truman Show*. The whole thing was very sad and painful, but not painful enough for me to wish I hadn't written the book.

Burrowing in

Writing memoir for me feels like I'm burrowing inside myself to a small place where all of this remains very much alive. Our stories are always somewhere within us. We need only to get still enough to look. Anne Sexton was once asked why she writes about such painful subjects and she responded that pain engraves a deeper memory. I think this is true. Though, of course, in time we can find light and humor even in the darkest moments.

I live a domestic, contented life. More and more I feel there's no contradiction and no delineation between my domestic life and my creative life. One can't exist without the other. There is this life and there is this driving need to dive into that place that then expands, and that world is as large and encompassing when I'm inside it as the world that's all around me.

Dani Shapiro's Wisdom for Memoir Writers

- Know your reasons for embarking on this memoir. If one of your reasons is revenge, stop. Wait. Writing from rage, or from the sting of betrayal, or whatever it might be that is motivating you, will produce an incoherent story. Be sure you have enough distance from your material so that you are able to think of yourself as a character.

- Don't worry about what people will think as you're writing a first draft. This manuscript will not magically fly from your desk and onto the shelves of your local bookstore. You'll have time to worry about people's feelings once you've gotten a draft down. But if you begin with this kind of fretting, you'll stop yourself before you've even started.

- Remember that you're telling a story. Not everything belongs. Understand that you may write other memoirs down the road, but come to know the frame around this story. Just because it happened to you does not make it relevant. Choose carefully what to put in and what to leave out.

CHAPTER FIFTEEN

David Sheff

*As a young child, my firstborn son, Nic, was happy and
excited about everything, kind and sincere and funny.
Parents like me monitor external barometers to tell us how
our kids are doing, and according to those, as Nic grew older,
he did well.*

—Opening, *Clean*, 2013

E ven before David Sheff's 2008 memoir, *Beautiful Boy*, became a number one *New York Times* bestseller, winning
him numerous awards and making him the go-to addiction guy
for desperate parents and media hounds alike, David Sheff was
a writer whose work you had probably read.

In his multidecade career as a journalist, David wrote seminal profiles of influencers like Steve Jobs, Ansel Adams, Jack
Nicholson, Michael Moore, Dr. Seuss, and Carl Sagan for
magazines like *Playboy*, *The New York Times Magazine*, *Wired*,
Rolling Stone, *Fortune*, and *Outside*. In 1980, he conducted the
last significant interview of John Lennon and Yoko Ono, about
which a *Los Angeles Times* columnist wrote, "David Sheff's sympathetic questions evoked so much of the Beatle past and of
Lennon's intellectual past and present and future plans that the

interview would hardly have been less engrossing and important even it if were not illuminated by tragedy."

David Sheff is a member of the largely unseen, largely unsung, and wildly underthanked cadre of hardworking, hardboiled reporters who do the best work in our infotainment news culture—going deep, going out on shaky limbs, going big, and then going home without many accolades or dollars to show for it. How good and how just, then, that David's turn to memoir earned him so much of both. Fans of David Sheff, new and old, can rejoice in knowing that this journeyman journalist gave us a beautiful book, and got his beautiful boy back in the process.

THE VITALS

Birthday: December 23, 1955

Born and raised: Boston, Massachusetts

Home now: Inverness, California

Family: Wife, Karen Barbour; children, Nic, 32; Jasper, 21; Daisy, 19

Schooling: University of California, Berkeley

Day job: Freelance journalist

Notable notes:

- *Beautiful Boy* was a #1 *New York Times* bestseller, was named 2008's Best Nonfiction Book by *Entertainment Weekly*, and won first place in the Barnes & Noble Discover Award in nonfiction.
- In 2009, David Sheff was listed among *Time* magazine's "100 Most Influential People in the World."
- David wrote an award-winning documentary about Stein-

beck's *Grapes of Wrath* and a radio show about Harper Lee, both for National Public Radio.

Facebook: https://www.facebook.com/david.sheff.3?fref=ts

Twitter: @david_sheff

Website: www.davidsheff.com

THE COLLECTED WORKS

Memoir

Beautiful Boy, 2008

Nonfiction

Game Over, 1993

China Dawn, 2002

All We Are Saying, 2000

Clean, 2013

Essays, Columns, Reviews (Partial Listing)

The New York Times

Playboy

Outside

Rolling Stone

Wired

David Sheff

Why I write about myself

Until I wrote my memoir, the books I wrote were intentional. I'd get an assignment for a magazine article and the piece would turn into a book, or I'd follow a subject of interest to me until I decided it was book-worthy.

Beautiful Boy wasn't a choice. I was dragged into that world, the world of drug addiction, when my eldest son became addicted to methamphetamine and other drugs. Part of the way I've always survived hard stuff is to write. So when Nic was addicted, when I didn't know where he was or what he was doing or whether he was dead or alive, I got through long nights writing, writing, writing.

When Nic had been doing better for a year and a half or so, I realized that we'd been completely blind-sighted. Our family was one of many who thought we were immune to addiction, but the hell we went through with Nic made me realize that no family is immune. That's what compelled me to tell our story—so people would know: yes, this *can* happen to you.

I wrote the story first as a piece for *The New York Times Magazine*. The reaction stunned me. I got such intimate letters from dozens and then hundreds and eventually thousands of people. Many of them asked, "How'd you get inside our home? You've described our situation exactly." Other people wrote me the details of what they were going through, even if they hadn't told anyone in their extended families. People felt compelled in some way to write to a stranger because we had this shared experience.

That's why I decided to write the memoir. When we suffer trauma, we need to know that we aren't alone. And we aren't.

What it was like to write about myself: razor blades

I can't even compare the journalism I'd done in the past to writing *Beautiful Boy*. They're totally different emotional experiences and processes.

When I'm writing as a journalist, I'm objective. There's a distance. I'm always compelled by what I'm writing, and by the people I meet while I'm reporting a story. What I'm working on always feels significant. But the memoir was life and death for me.

There was no separation at all. Writing felt like slitting my wrist with a razor, bloodletting. It was visceral. It was revelatory sometimes. It was about trying to make sense of what was chaos in my brain and in our lives. It was also a kind of purging, a way of dealing with years of overwhelming emotion.

It cut me, and it changed me

I still do objective journalism, but the process of writing *Beautiful Boy* changed me as a writer. I learned more about how to tell a story. Everything hung on the structure of our journey as a family. That felt so compelling to me, and I relied on the unfolding chronology more than I usually do.

There was a point when I realized that I was crossing a line between personal and professional reporting. I was no longer writing only as a journalist. I did the reporting as a journalist, but I wasn't objective about this subject. I've become someone who cares so deeply, and is so deeply associated with people struggling with mental illness, my journalism has been replaced by advocacy.

A similar thing happened in April 1995, when I wrote about joint custody of my son for *The New York Times Magazine*. That was also a personal piece. It was my reaction to my traumatic divorce and a draconian custody agreement that ended up being tragic for my son. That piece also came from a place of pain. I was struggling to understand more deeply a personal situation that also affects many other people. Divorcing parents rationalize the trauma we inflict on our kids.

Those pieces have a different quality. They have a power that's different from other things I write. It comes from somewhere else. My take on them is not objective at all.

At first the distinction between journalism and memoir was confusing to me. I'm a journalist by training. There are plenty of things I write about that I'm not objective about: the death penalty, the prison system, injustices done to those who can least afford them. But as a journalist, no matter my personal view, I write about those subjects with as much objectivity as I can muster. I've interviewed people whose politics I agree with, like Barney Frank, Gore Vidal, Dan Savage, Salman Rushdie, Ai Weiwei, and David Hockney. But still, as a journalist I asked the tough questions that needed to be asked. I challenged them on their views.

I've also interviewed people whose politics I abhor. Bill O'Reilly of Fox News, for example. I've interviewed people on the far right whose views I strongly, strongly disagree with. That made it easier to ask hard questions, but I was fair—at least I tried to be. In my introductions to those interviews I wrote about their work objectively, quoting people on both sides of contentious issues.

One memoir is enough

I loved writing the memoir. It's a powerful form that involved deep and continuous and often painful introspection, copping to stuff that I didn't want to admit to myself, and wrestling with things about myself that I didn't want to acknowledge or accept. It was healing. Despite that—or maybe because of that—I won't be writing another memoir.

I did write a personal piece for *Time* that was addiction related, about my one and only drug deal, which happened when
I was in college. I barely escaped unscathed. Because of the
quantity of drugs I had, I would have ended up in prison for
twenty years minimum. I included my own story in the context
of an article about mandatory minimum sentencing, talking
about people who are in prison for crimes far less serious than
mine. I used my own story to raise questions about justice and
about people making stupid mistakes like I did—mistakes with
potentially life-altering consequences.

No family member was harmed in the making of this book

It's one thing to write a book about yourself, but I hear from
people all the time asking me if it's okay to write a memoir
about their families. Everyone has a story to tell, and so many
people are inspired to tell it. I always encourage people to
write—to write like hell—to do it for themselves. Only later
should they contemplate the potential consequences if they
were to publish their work. There are two separate issues here.
One is about the value of the process of writing our own stories.
The other is about going public by publishing it. It's a really,
really, really important distinction. I'd call into question anyone who is writing a memoir without examining it thoroughly
and repeatedly. Here's where I came down. I wouldn't have
written a word if I didn't have the support and encouragement
of everyone in my family. My two younger kids were too young
to be involved in the decision, but my wife and I talked a lot
about the implications for them. Mostly I wanted Nic to feel

100 percent okay about being exposed in this way. He embraced it fully. He said the books that helped him grow up were memoirs, people who went through hell and wrote about it with searing honesty.

I talked to Nic's mom. I talked to my parents. I talked to everyone who could be affected, and I asked them to read the manuscript before I published it. When you go through something like Nic's addiction, everyone involved is hurt so intensely. It was brutally traumatic for everybody involved. I would never want to inflict any more pain on anyone.

If I'd come to the conclusion that publishing the story would have injured anyone, I wouldn't have done it. If there was a paragraph that was uncomfortable to somebody, I took it out.

When I'm doing objective journalism, it's no-holds-barred. Whatever advances the story. But the memoir was about the lives of people I adore. Most people don't write memoirs about having a nice walk on the beach or sitting in the garden. There's usually enormous pain that leads to memoir. And I felt strongly that I didn't want to hurt people more than they'd already been hurt.

It was tricky, of course. I scrutinized every word in the book. I'd stay up in the middle of the night agonizing over whether to include something. I went over and over every sentence until I was confident that nothing would come back to haunt anyone.

In the end, everyone agreed it was empowering to the people in the book, even my younger kids. It helped them understand what they went through when they were little. You never, ever know for sure, but I did everything I could to include only positive, useful healing in the book. And that's what happened.

What concerns me is that a lot of the time, parents are writing about their sixteen-year-old children, and you can't rely on a sixteen-year-old's permission. They're easily influenced and can't necessarily think about the long-term consequences of their decisions. Nic was older and had already committed to speaking openly about his addiction in his book, *Tweak*.

I get the feeling that some people are so determined to tell their own story that they'll say they want permission but they don't. They're determined to write that book, and they'll trample over people who get in their way. I think that's dangerous, especially when you're talking about kids.

There were two principles that I followed. One was, Hurt no one. I know, I know, that sounds like the Google motto, "Do no evil."

The other principle broke down into two categories: one about me, and one about everyone else I wrote about. If there was something I was afraid of telling about myself—because I was embarrassed, or afraid of judgment—I determined at the beginning that I was going to tell it.

That was hard sometimes. My editor would say, "You don't have to include those three pages," but I'd include them. Once I'd committed to telling the truth, I decided to do exactly that, except where someone else would be hurt by it. That was the second category. If I had doubts about the impact of a story on anyone else in the book, I deleted it unless I got their permission to include it.

Deciding what and what not to include about Nic was harder. He was the most vulnerable. I was telling the story of my son who'd become a drug addict. There's judgment and shame and blame around addiction. I was exposing him, and there are people who don't get jobs because of addiction. Those judgments are changing, as people begin to understand that it's an illness, but addicts are still often treated differently.

In my *Times* story about Nic, I'd written about what a great, smart kid he was, and noted that he'd written for his high school newspaper and won the national Ernest Hemingway Writing Award for high school journalists. At the time I was deciding whether to write *Beautiful Boy*, I got a call from an editor at Simon & Schuster, asking if Nic would consider writing a memoir.

Nic was thrilled, of course. Memoirs got him through his childhood. He loved the idea that in writing a memoir, you don't have to keep secrets. You can reveal yourself. There's a saying in AA, "You're as sick as your secrets." There's an intensely powerful freedom when you decide you're not going to keep secrets anymore.

Nic's version of the same experience was so much more revelatory than mine. Once he decided to write his memoir I was given a lot more license with mine. It wasn't just that he'd given me permission to tell the story, but he'd determined to tell it, too. It became a family joke, that my wife would write about being the stepmother in a situation like this, and then Daisy and Jasper could both write their own memoirs, and it would become a family tradition.

The memoir asked to be written

My article came out in the *Times* in 2008. My editor said they got more letters in response to it than they'd gotten in a long,

long time. The letters were forwarded to me and I was completely stunned by them, and moved by them, and in tears over them. I was working on a business book at the time, about architecture and LEGO toys and the impact on little kids. But the reaction to the *Times* article showed me that more needed to be written about addiction.

In the aftermath of the article, I decided I'd write *Beautiful Boy*, and then I'd go back to writing the architecture book. Within the first week of the article coming out, Nic was talking to Simon & Schuster about writing his own memoir. It all happened at once.

And then Nic relapsed. It happened a couple of times. He said the only thing that kept him from going over the edge and killing himself was this idea that he was writing a book—he had something to say. Maybe he had value.

He always had wanted to be a writer. His heroes were writers. And he kept writing even when he was out of his mind on drugs. He'd send stuff to our agent, Binky Urban, and to his editor, and they'd call him up and say, "Nic, this makes no sense. You really are in trouble. You need to get help." Then he'd get clean again and write more.

The memoir for him was part of the roller coaster of the process that led him finally to recovery. And for me, too. Nic would be doing fine, and writing, and then he'd crash and burn again. I kept writing—as I said, the process was cathartic, about surviving a haunted night—but I knew all along that I wouldn't publish the memoir unless Nic was okay. Some people write memoirs ten, twenty, fifty years later, about growing up and how hard it was. There's distance there, there's time to reflect and to have already processed the experiences. But that's not what happened in our case. You couldn't separate the writing from living this nightmare.

It was hell. But from it came hope

The best thing to come out of the memoir was the connection to people who read it and felt an enormous relief to know they weren't alone. I've become very close with lots of people I never would have met. Not a day goes by that I don't hear from someone telling me his or her own story.

Maybe some people would think this is a negative thing, but when I go into a room, I don't have to start with small talk. If people have read the book, they know a hell of a lot about me. Maybe too much, but . . . there's not a lot of wasted time, not a lot of sitting around talking about the weather. Immediately people tell me about their own or a loved one's addiction, a difficult divorce, or of illness, loss, or pain they've endured. There are people who tell me about abuse, psychological disorders, mental illness in someone they love, accidents, losses in their lives. People will say, "I'm sure you hear this all the time; I'm sorry to burden you." But it doesn't feel like a burden. It feels like an intimate connection. I feel honored that people trust me to talk about stuff they wouldn't say to others. It's a gift.

Continuing the conversation, including inside our family, has been really valuable to all of us. Daisy and Jasper have found that it's been a connection to people, too. Daisy's now nineteen, and Jasper's twenty-one. Nic is thirty-two. Jasper had this amazing experience. He was on a camping trip with a close friend shortly after the book came out. The two of them were sitting up through a windy night in Yosemite, and the boy told him something he hadn't told anybody. The boy said, "I read your brother's story. I'm so sorry you're going through this. My brother tried to kill himself, and no one in my family wants to talk about it."

The unconscious speaks

We write from intention to a point, but there's also a level that comes out that's unconscious. When I read memoirs I can see the intended word, but also deeply into the writer, sometimes in ways the writer doesn't intend. Sometimes it increases my respect for them and my compassion, and sometimes I feel a disingenuousness between them and the words on the page.

What people got from my memoir is in part what I intended them to get, but probably also some that I didn't intend. Some people maybe get to the end of the book, and because it has an optimistic ending, they feel our family went off into the sunset and all has been easy and light-filled. Nic's great; it's all great; it's all easy and lovely now. I tried to make clear that that's not how life works. But people want to know how to get where we are—healed after the trauma that went on for years. We go on struggling. Yes, there's joy and a closeness that comes from surviving a war together, but humans are fraught and frail. Life is hard. It doesn't end on the last page of a memoir.

David Sheff's Wisdom for Memoir Writers

- Whatever you write in a memoir, whatever effect it has, you've got to live with it forever. Don't hurt people.

- Anne Lamott's *Bird by Bird* is an incredibly valuable tool for all writers, and memoir writers in particular—a bible. Borrowing from Anne: Write a shitty first draft. Spill it all, then go back and fix it later. The prospect of writing a book can be overwhelming and paralyzing. As the title suggests, take it bird by bird—a single story, moment, or revelation at a time.

- Don't take writing a memoir lightly. Take your time. Do your work. Second-guess and third-guess yourself in terms of what to keep and what to cut. Accept nothing short of the truth.

- If what you're writing about wasn't intense, you wouldn't be writing about it. Writing a memoir can dredge up every awful feeling all over again. Make sure you have the support you need to make it through.

CHAPTER SIXTEEN

Darin Strauss

Half my life ago, I killed a girl.

I had just turned eighteen, and when you drive in new post-adolescence, you drive with friends. We were headed to shoot a few rounds of putt-putt. It was May 1988. The breeze did its open-window work on the hair behind my neck and ears.

—Opening, *Half a Life*, 2010

⁂

What a way to start a memoir: "Half my life ago, I killed a girl."

All was well, more than well, in Darin Strauss's life. He was married with twins on the way, and he'd published three novels, and all of them were hits. He'd won a Guggenheim Fellowship, his novels had been widely reviewed and praised and named as various "Best ofs," and . . .

"I had this secret, kept from the world," Darin told me, speaking of the accident in which he'd "killed a girl." "It had formed me. It had malformed me." And so he chose to write his first memoir—also his last, he says.

The critical and commercial success of Darin Strauss's

memoir seems proof that memoirists need not choose between art and therapy when practicing their craft. A memoir can be a sort of literary support group, led by an experienced expert who shares his own trauma for the benefit of all concerned.

THE VITALS

Birthday: March 1, 1970

Born and raised: Roslyn Harbor, Long Island, New York

Home now: Brooklyn, New York

Family: Married to Susannah Meadows; identical twin sons

Schooling: Tufts University; New York University

Day job: Professor in New York University's creative writing program

Notable notes:

- *Chang and Eng*, Darin's first novel, was a *Los Angeles Times* and *Newsweek* Best Book of the Year. Darin and Gary Oldman are adapting the novel for film.
- After publication of his second novel, *The Real McCoy*, which was a *New York Times* Notable Book for 2002, Darin won a Guggenheim Fellowship in Fiction Writing.
- *Half a Life* won the National Book Critics Circle Award.

Facebook: https://www.facebook.com/darin.strauss?fref=ts

Twitter: @Darinstrauss

Website: www.darinstrauss.com

THE COLLECTED WORKS

Memoir

Half a Life, 2010

Novels

Chang and Eng, 2000

The Real McCoy, 2002

More Than It Hurts You, 2008

Darin Strauss

Why I write about myself

I thought I'd never write nonfiction. Nonfiction wasn't my thing. But I had this secret that I'd kept from the world, and for some reason, at a certain moment, I felt I needed to transform that secret into print.

I was thirty-six. My wife was pregnant with our kids. I'd lived with the accident exactly as long as I had before it. The confluence of those events returned me to that afternoon; I had a more visceral understanding of what it would be like to lose a child. The events of the book had happened exactly half my life earlier. They had formed me. They had malformed me. It was time to face the past. And the way I deal with things, and figure out what I actually feel about them, is to put them to paper.

As someone who follows Updike's dictum ("A writer's responsibility is to get published"), I suppose it was pretty much inevitable. I teach storytelling, and I always tell my students that if they have a story to tell, it's their responsibility to tell it.

I think a memoirist's brain acts out the coal-to-diamond

process. A story puts pressure on the brain; the book is what comes out.

I wrote three books before I was ready to tell this story. I would have been unable to write *Half a Life* at eighteen—at twenty-five—at thirty—had someone tried forcing me to. Even when I thought I was ready, the execution was tough. I couldn't expose half of myself. I had to jump in and expose everything.

I think that's why there's a general sense among writers that memoirs are less good than novels. It's not that the best memoirs are worse than the best novels; that's not true. But there are fewer excellent memoirs. Why? When they fail, often it's because you can sense some protection in every paragraph. The author has two purposes: one, to tell the story; two, to make himself look good, to protect himself. Generally, that's not something you feel in a novel. Which is to say, a novelist isn't telling a story while protecting his characters. You have to throw personal concerns out the window if you write a memoir.

That's why I'd never write another memoir. There's still stuff in my life I'm not comfortable writing about. I know now it takes boldness to write a good memoir; I don't want to be bold all the time. With *Half a Life*, I tried to have the bravery to write about this one thing fully. I didn't want to protect myself, and I wouldn't be so unguarded next time because there are other things to protect besides oneself. There are relationships I want to protect, so I won't write about fatherhood or marriage. I don't want to hurt my relationships with my wife or my kids.

My twenty-page book

I just wanted to write about the incident, not about anything beyond that. I had no intention of writing a full book. In particular, I didn't want to write an autobiography in which I talked about myself in different contexts. Me at six, going to kindergarten; me at forty, learning to be a dad. Who'd care? The one interesting detail of my life—the one book-worthy detail—was the accident.

Initially, *Half a Life* was going to be a thirty- to forty-page book. It'd focus just on that accident, for just the amount of space I needed to focus on it. My publisher said, "That's not possible—you can't do a book that short." I said, "What if it was about just the incident?" My publisher said, "Pad it out with memories," and crap like that. I said, "That's not what I want to do with this particular story. That would be disrespectful." I wasn't going to do it.

Then Dave Eggers said *McSweeney's* would do a thirty-page book if I wanted. Great—sign me up! But in the writing I went on longer than I thought I would. Just because I felt this freedom to write only what I wanted to write, it turned out to be a two-hundred-page book

It didn't feel good

I'm a hider. It felt weird to write about myself. It was profoundly uncomfortable.

In particular, the accident at the heart of the book was something about which I was very unwilling to talk to people, even in a personal way. Add to that my generally private nature and you have a reluctant memoirist. It would have been much easier to tell the story if I could hide behind the wall of my imagination. But that felt wrong and disrespectful and I couldn't do it.

There were other challenges, too. While I was writing *Half a Life*, I worried about everything I worry about when I'm writing fiction. Authenticity. Honesty. Artfulness. Being respectful. The limits of my talent.

With the memoir, I also worried about remembering right. I did the best I could with my memories. I wanted the book to be as accurate as I could make it. I didn't want to invent stuff.

I once talked to Dani Shapiro about truth and memory in memoir. We agreed that remembering the best you can is okay, as long as you're not lying. A memoir is not a history book. It's a record of your life as you remember it. You could write the same story every ten years, and each book might be less accurate than the last—but the accuracy won't necessarily determine which is a better book. We don't judge memoirs by that criterion.

What makes a memoir isn't just what you remember; it's your insights about what you remember. Again, a twenty-year-old's memoir might be more accurate in terms of the details, but it won't be better than a sixty-year-old's memoir, because the older author will likely have more insights that put the story in a larger context.

I'd rather read a great writer's shaky recollection than a fourteen-year-old's exact recollection.

And then it felt better

The anxiety went away once I realized that I had to look at writing a memoir the same way I write a novel—that this was a story about a character who's flawed, and all I had to do was expose that character, flaws and all.

Now when I teach memoir, I tell my students to change the "I" to a "she"; this makes it easier. It gives the requisite distance. How much easier it is to say "she is messing up here, and is unlikable" than "I am . . ."

If you write your character that way—if you actually do a word replace—it frees you to write with an honesty that's pretty hard to come by otherwise.

I know I did my best to be authentic, and I know I really was honest. Those are the things I stand by. I don't know about the art of it; I'm a terrible judge of my own work after I'm done with it. But I'm proud of the book.

A flawed character: me

When the book was being edited, the editors kept telling me to change things because they made me look bad. I said, "That's how I know I'm doing something right and the book is working. The only justification for doing a book like this is to tell the truth about yourself. There's no moral justification for writing a book to make yourself look good."

For example, the first scene in the book is the accident. I was in shock. Everyone was standing around the cars. Some pretty young girls came out of their cars, and I was flirting with them. The editors said, "You have to take that out. It makes you look bad."

I'm aware that flirting at the accident scene doesn't make me look good. But I was writing the book for someone who went through a similar thing. In real life, we do inappropriate things at inappropriate times. If I didn't tell the truth in order to make myself look better than I was, the book might make that person feel worse about himself. Someone who did something inappropriate might think, I went through something, and I didn't handle it as well as this guy.

That convinced me to emphasize my flaws. Anywhere I had selfish, inappropriate thoughts, I kept them all in the book. Every chance I got, I made myself look bad. If nonfiction is any good, it has to be harder on the protagonist than on anybody else. The problem with so many memoirs is that they're propaganda. It's an argument for the defense. I wanted to write an argument for the prosecution.

We have the right to privacy as Americans, but not as memoirists. I very jealously guard my privacy when it comes to the parts of my life I choose not to write about. But once I write about something, I can't then say I won't talk about that. If you're going to write a memoir and you're not going to talk about what makes it painful with 100 percent honesty, I'm not going to waste my time reading it.

No one's forcing you to talk about this stuff, so don't think you can broach a subject that no one's asking you to broach, and then demand that walls be put around it at the same time.

Amy Hempel tells a good story about when she was in a beginning workshop with Gordon Lish. He had the class write about the one thing that most embarrassed them. The only restriction was that you had to write it as honestly as possible. She said that out of that class of fifteen people, seven or eight published pieces they wrote in that class. If you write something honestly, it'll be worth reading. If you don't, it doesn't matter how good a writer you are. The reader will feel it.

Therapeutic?

I held a different standard for the other characters in the book. The girl in the book, she's dead. I wanted to protect her and her family. There were things I left out about her and them. Protecting her memory, leaving out these things, made me look worse, but I felt I had no moral choice.

Before I wrote about it—before I faced it—I knew that my representation of the accident wasn't admirable in any way. It was the opposite. I was searching for the wrong answers. Being in denial isn't really the best way to learn to deal with something terrible.

Writing the book was completely therapeutic. William Gass says if writing is cathartic, you're not doing it right, because writing well is so hard that you don't have time for catharsis. Well, either I did it wrong or Gass was wrong, because writing *Half a Life* was cathartic for me.

I think Gass was wrong. When you write your own story, you have to face it in order to make decisions about how you're going to tell it, what to emphasize, what's important. Those things that help us shape the story also help us shape our understanding of the events we're writing about. I found it very advantageous in dealing with them.

Keep those cards and letters coming

When you write fiction, people don't write you as often, and when they do, it's: "I liked it." Or: "I didn't like it." With a personal story, often people feel compelled to share their own stories. I must have gotten a thousand such stories. I'd love to do a book of these e-mails: people baring their most personal wounds, in the most beautiful ways. Not beautiful because they're well crafted, necessarily. But the honesty and emotion—it floored me.

I got a Guggenheim. It helped

Some writers don't like having an advance. It puts them under too much pressure. But knowing I'll be published again lets me stop worrying about that, at least.

Getting a big award for my memoir was really gratifying. You put yourself out there, and it's a little scary. I talked a big game after it was published, but I was also pretty worried about it. I thought, I did sort of make myself look bad. Maybe I should have listened to my editor. Maybe people will come after me. To have the memoir do well was a relief—even more so than other books. To get bad reviews for a novel sucks. But bad reviews for a memoir feel exponentially worse, because they can be about you as a person.

Darin Strauss's Wisdom for Memoir Writers

- Write the first draft of your memoir in third person, not first. That'll make it easier for you to be tough on yourself, as you should be.
- If you commit to a memoir, you have to commit fully. If there's stuff you want to avoid saying, write a different book.

CHAPTER SEVENTEEN

Cheryl Strayed

The trees were tall, but I was taller, standing above them on a steep mountain slope in northern California. Moments before, I'd removed my hiking boots and the left one had fallen into those trees, first catapulting into the air when my enormous backpack toppled onto it, then skittering across the gravelly trail and flying over the edge.

—Opening, *Wild*, 2012

High school basketball players shoot at their NBA dreams, bit actresses rehearse their Oscar acceptance speeches, and writers write, imagining each book as a runaway bestseller, soon to be a major motion picture, completing the transformation from starving artist to literary celebrity.

No one would buy lottery tickets if someone didn't win big every once in a while. Without the occasional surprise blockbuster, writers would have no excuse to believe that even if the last book failed to deliver wealth and fame, the next one will.

Cheryl Strayed is one of a tiny handful of writers for whom that fantasy became reality—and one of an even tinier handful who not only earned their success, but also manage to wear it gracefully. Until her second book, *Wild*, was optioned for film by Reese Witherspoon, landed at the top of the *New York Times* bestseller list, and was an Oprah's Book Club 2.01 pick, Cheryl was a member of the literary 99 percent. She won a few prizes and had a few short stories included in prestigious collections and wrote essays for some well-known publications, but she struggled to pay her bills and feel her work was worthwhile, as most writers—published and unpublished—do. Her 2006 novel, *Torch*, was positively reviewed but didn't garner exceptional sales. Her pseudonymous, unpaid column for *The Rumpus*, Dear Sugar, was wildly popular, but no one knew who Sugar was until six weeks before *Wild* was published.

And then *Wild* hit with the velocity of an asteroid plummeting to earth, and everything changed for Cheryl Strayed, except who she is: the hiker who kept going when her boot fell off the mountain; the humble heart and mind behind the sassy advice columnist Sugar; the talented, dedicated, generous writer who does much for many, including her adoring readers.

"Strayed has found the success most people will never know," Jason Diamond wrote in *Flavorwire* in April 2014, "but she keeps working like she still has something to prove. It's something that keeps readers interested, and even the snobbiest writers can still appreciate her work ethic."

THE VITALS

Birthday: September 17, 1968

Born and raised: Born in Pennsylvania, raised in Minnesota.

Home now: Portland, Oregon

Family: Husband Brian Lindstrom; children ages nine and ten

Schooling: BA, University of Minnesota; MFA in fiction writing, Syracuse University

Day job: Nope

Notable notes:

- Cheryl was born in a small mining town in central Pennsylvania, then moved to Minnesota when she was six. From age twelve onward, she lived with her mother, stepfather, sister, and brother in a cabin in northern Minnesota on forty acres—a few of those years with no running water or electricity, and all of those years with no indoor toilet.
- The movie adaptation of *Wild* was released in December 2014. Reese Witherspoon played Cheryl.
- Cheryl's books have been translated into more than thirty languages worldwide.

Facebook: https://www.facebook.com/CherylStrayed.Author

Twitter: @CherylStrayed

Website: www.cherylstrayed.com

THE COLLECTED WORKS

Novel

Torch, 2006

Nonfiction

Tiny Beautiful Things, 2012

Memoir

Wild, 2012

Essays, Columns, Stories (Partial Listing)

The Sun

The Rumpus

The Best American Essays, 2000, 2003, 2013, and 2015

The Missouri Review

Creative Nonfiction

Cheryl Strayed

Why I write about myself

Since I write both fiction and nonfiction, I'm always asking myself if material I have from my own life would be best used in a novel or a memoir or a short story or an essay. I was moved to write *Wild* as a memoir because I thought that was the best way to tell that particular story.

Each genre offers a different thing. In fiction, you aren't bound by the things that actually happened. You can begin there and then let the story go wherever you want. Memoir is bound by what actually happened—or at least by the writer's memory and interpretation of what happened—but there's a great amount of power present in reading something where the writer is standing right there behind the sentences, saying, "This is true."

I felt that the story I told in *Wild* best fit that form and benefited from that position. On the other hand, my first novel, *Torch*, is a book in which I drew on my life but also made lots of things up and I think that was the best decision, too.

What's universal about my life

Pretty early on I learned that for better or worse I was going to use my life in my writing, whether in fiction or nonfiction. Not because I think my life is more interesting than anyone else's, but rather I was going to use the self as a means to write stories that feel universal.

The only way I know how to do that is to plumb the depths of my own heart, mind, body, and spirit. So I had to make myself ready for a life in which I share the most private parts of myself with the public. I didn't learn how to do that all at once. It's a muscle you work and build over time.

I worry about all the usual stuff every writer worries about—wanting people to like me and my work, wanting to not hurt or infuriate others when I write about them—but mostly I worry about writing well.

I aspire to greatness. I want to write literature that moves people, that looks them in the eye and reaches into their guts. My biggest worry is fulfilling the mission of literature, which is to tell us what it means to be human.

I don't feel inhibited when I'm really working. When I'm working I'm split open and fearless. I feel inhibited when I spin my wheels wondering what others will think of my work. I'm fueled by the desire to give beauty and truth to the world via the sentences I construct. I really want that in this deep, core, essential way. There's an ache inside me that's soothed only by writing.

Shield the ones you love

I'm extremely candid about myself in my writing, but I protect others as much as I can. It isn't my right to expose people or hurt them or embarrass them.

Of course, that doesn't mean that no one has ever felt hurt or exposed or embarrassed by what I wrote about them, but I'm very, very mindful of how to avoid that as often as possible. I write with compassion, even about people who've done me wrong. I'm constantly questioning myself when I write about others. I write only what must be known as it relates to me.

Me? Not so much . . .

I don't impose privacy parameters in my writing about myself. Writing isn't about privacy. It's about the opposite of that. It's about truth.

I try to go one or two sentences beyond what I feel safe saying. Honestly, that's where it's at—the one sentence that makes you bolt out of your chair because after you write it you feel someone lit your hands on fire.

I'm not saying the secret is writing down every terrible thing that has happened to you. I'm not talking about confession. I'm talking about necessity, about telling the deepest truth at the right moment and being in command of that.

I think a lot of people get those two things confused. They think if they had a trauma or a drama or took a wonderful trip they've got a book, but that's not art. As Sugar I wrote, "Art isn't anecdote, it's the consciousness we bring to bear on the stories we tell." I think it's a really key point. I'm open and vulnerable in the service of the work, not because I want to expose myself and rely on the shock of that exposure.

. . . except in the real world

In the work I don't protect my privacy, but I do try to protect my privacy as the human behind the work.

Many readers feel they know me after they've read one of my books. I'm deeply flattered and touched by that, but I sometimes need to set boundaries. At my events I've had people stand up in front of an audience of a thousand people and ask if I've cheated on my husband. They think that because I've written about my experiences with infidelity and sex, my entire life is up for discussion. But it isn't.

I decide what I make public through my work. I perform intimacy through my writing, but that doesn't mean I'm intimate with everyone who reads it. When I say "perform," I don't mean it's fake—in fact it's incredibly authentic. I mean the way I'm raw and open in my writing is not an accident. It's a crafted, considered effort. It's something I've made with a great amount of intention and consciousness.

A shorter way of saying this is there's a big difference between feeling like you're my best friend because you identified with my work and being my best friend.

Shock and awe

The best thing that has happened as a result of publishing *Wild* is hearing people tell me their lives have been changed or saved by it.

I've heard their stories every day since *Wild* was published and I'll never get over how that feels. It means a lot to me, no matter how many times I hear it. Thousands—literally thousands—of people have told me that in reading *Wild* they realized their life is exactly like mine. How can that be? And yet, it is.

I have felt changed and saved by books by other people, so I'm deeply moved that *Wild* has done the same for so many others. I'm grateful, humbled, and awed.

Success and writing

The success of *Wild* hasn't changed my writing or the way I think of myself as a writer, though I do feel a greater sense of being onstage.

Many people are waiting for my next book, and that's both exhilarating and strange to me. If I let that get into my head too much it stresses me out because the people pleaser in me wants to write a book that will make everyone happy. Of course I can't write that book. Or at least I can't do it intentionally.

When I was writing *Wild* I wasn't thinking it was going to be a blockbuster. I was thinking I was writing the best possible book I could write at that moment in my life. If all goes well, I will think the same thing about every book I write for the rest of my life. Anything else is a delusion.

What you get isn't all there is to see

Words that are often used to describe my work are "raw" and "brave." I think that's because I'm rather fearless in my work when it comes to self-exposure. And yet I think sometimes people don't realize that in fact I don't always tell everything.

My work doesn't hinge on shock value. I tell only what needs to be told for the work to reach its full potential. I'm not interested in confession. I'm interested in revelation.

When I'm reading, I don't want to know every terrible thing that happened to the author just for the sake of knowing. I want to know what meaning he or she made of what happened. I want to be dazzled by the language, the structure, the moment. It takes time to develop that as a writer. It takes an apprenticeship to the craft. I'm old-school that way.

What love's got to do with it

I don't think the morality of writing memoir is much different from the morality of writing fiction.

Both real-life and imaginary people become characters on the page. We owe it to them to give them the benefit of the doubt, to be kind but candid, to reveal their complexities and points of view.

There are some people who would be hurt if I portrayed them honestly in my work and so I don't portray them, because not hurting them is more important to me than anything I want to write. In other cases, I've chosen the other path, but rarely—and really only in the case of my father. I'm sure he hates what I've written about him. Although I take no pleasure in whatever negative emotions he may feel when reading my work, I feel it's my right to write about my life and his place in it.

You have to think about the personal consequences of writing about others on a case-by-case basis. If there's going to be a price to pay for writing about someone, it's a valid question to ask if you're willing to pay it. Sometimes you are; other times you aren't. There is no one answer to this question. You just have to do your best to write with good intentions, which is to say with love.

Cheryl Strayed's Wisdom for Memoir Writers

- The most powerful strand in memoir is not expressing your originality. It's tapping into your universality. This isn't to say you shouldn't be original in your writing—you are the only one who can write that universal experience in just that way. Trust that.

- Know that the writing will lead you into places you can't imagine you'll go. In my experience, writing comes from a place beneath intellectual consciousness. The only way to get to that place is by writing. Trust the magic of that process.

- Good writing is built on craft and heart. Another way of saying it is you must do your work and it must cost you everything to do it.

Chapter Eighteen

Ayelet Waldman

*The morning after my wedding, my husband, Michael, and I
were lying on a vast expanse of white linen in the bridal suite
of Berkeley's oldest hotel, engaging in a romantic tradition of
newlyweds the world over: counting our loot. Sifting through
the checks, I said, "What's with the multiples of eighteen?"*

—Opening, *Bad Mother*, 2009

A yelet Waldman's career as a memoirist might be best described by the old saw "The best defense is a good offense."
Some writers, including a few who say so in these pages,
regret or resent or rail against the stereotype of memoirists as
self-obsessed, navel-gazing narcissists armed with Internet
connections and/or book deals. Waldman embraces the cri-
tique. She doesn't wait for *Gawker* to accuse her of loving her
husband more than she loves her kids; she writes an essay detailing why that's true—in the *New York Times*, no less. She
doesn't cry "off-limits" when asked about her suicidal tenden-
cies; she writes a blog post about staring down the pill bottles
in the family medicine cabinet. Instead of denying her mental
illness, she says, "The upside of being bipolar is that it makes
you really productive."

Having been berated by an astonishingly diverse assortment of readers for an impressively long list of transgressions—Oprah's audience members, who called her a selfish hussy; mommy bloggers, who called her an abusive mother; hipster gossip columnists, who accused her of feigning self-awareness to build her brand; and un-fans of her column on Salon.com, who called her pretty much every bad name in the book—Ayelet's response was to publish a memoir called *Bad Mother: A Chronicle of Maternal Crimes, Minor Calamities, and Occasional Moments of Grace.*

Ayelet Waldman doesn't just get hate mail. She also gets letters thanking her for the validation and reassurance her fans derive from her writing. Having observed Ayelet's role in our shared Berkeley community, and at risk of jeopardizing her reputation as a hard-ass, take-no-prisoners, truth-telling opportunist, I can personally assure you that calling Ayelet Waldman's proclivity for disclosure "a publicity stunt" is like accusing a canary of having ulterior motives when she sings inside a mine. For personal, political, and literary reasons, I wouldn't want to live in a world without Ayelet Waldman. Would you?

THE VITALS

Birthday: December 11, 1964

Born and raised: Jerusalem; Washington, DC; Montreal; Rhode Island; New Jersey

Home now: Berkeley, California

Family: Married to Michael Chabon since 1993; children Sophie (b. 1994), Ezekiel (b. 1997), Ida-Rose (b. 2001), and Abraham (b. 2003)

Schooling: Wesleyan University; Harvard Law School

Day job: Nope

Notable notes:

- Although Ayelet was never bat mitzvahed, she attended Hebrew school and Jewish summer camps and lived on a kibbutz for one year of high school.
- "When I write about mental illness," she says, "I feel queasy and ashamed, but I also feel really strongly that I shouldn't feel this way, that this is a disease, like diabetes."
- Ayelet was a classmate of Barack Obama's at Harvard Law School; she was a major fund-raiser for his presidential campaigns.

Facebook: https://www.facebook.com/ayeletwaldman?fref=ts

Twitter: @ayeletw

Website: www.ayeletwaldman.com

THE COLLECTED WORKS

Novels

Mommy-Track Mystery series, 2000–06

Daughter's Keeper, 2003

Love and Other Impossible Pursuits, 2006

Red Hook Road, 2010

Love & Treasure, 2013

Memoir

Bad Mother, 2009

Essays, Features (Partial Listing)

Harper's Bazaar

New York

The New York Times

Salon.com

Ayelet Waldman

Why I write about myself

I never decided to write a memoir. There was no cathartic moment. It just happened. At some point I realized that I had more to say about the subject of motherhood than could fit into an essay or even a few essays. Once I started working on it, I looked back at my previously published work and realized that not only was this all of a piece, but that the various pieces, along with the new material I was generating, constituted a memoir. But even at that moment I never consciously decided to engage in the process of self-revelation. I was much more focused on the book itself—its structure and the points it was making.

The process of writing about myself began in that most prosaic of ways: with a blog. I'd been writing these mommy mysteries, one after another, on a rigid schedule, and I decided to take six weeks off. As it turned out, though I'd always thought of myself as a somewhat lazy person, when it came down to it, I was incapable of taking time off. So there I was, desperate to write, but determined not to start a new book. And here was this new(ish) medium, the blog, just waiting for me to indulge my hypergraphia. Writing the blog was the first time I'd really written about myself in a way that wasn't disguised by the project of writing fiction.

One of the first important posts I wrote was about my second-term abortion. The results of writing about that were so dramatic, both in terms of how I felt exposing this secret and in terms of the reactions I got from readers, that I found myself thinking, Oh, this is a *thing*. This satisfies a personal need for expression in a way that fiction doesn't, both in a positive way and in a negative way. And more important, there's a public purpose to this in a way that there isn't to fiction.

I've always been, in some senses, a political writer. Or at least a writer who doesn't shy away from political subject matter. Even my silly little murder mysteries always had some underlying theme; the most obvious being the eternal, doomed struggle to "balance" work and motherhood. But the blog gave me a way to write very specifically about things I cared about. It gave me a forum to expose injustice in the legal system, the penal system, and every other wrong I was incensed about.

In my first post I wrote about a teenager who'd been imprisoned for statutory rape because he had a consensual relationship with another teen. This poor kid was sentenced to ten years. The post was good, effective. It made its point. But it wasn't personal. Afterward I wondered if I'd lost the opportunity to reach more people by shying away from personal revelation. I wondered, if I had allowed myself to be more self-revelatory, would more people have seen the piece, and been exposed to the larger, political point that I was trying to make? Could I have been more effective at achieving social change if I'd used memoir rather than traditional reportorial methods? Personal stories make people change their minds and their awareness in a way that pure advocacy doesn't.

Someone at *Salon* saw the abortion piece on my blog, and they asked to put it up on their site. A month later they asked me to write a regular column. At this point I had grown sick of the blog. I wanted to continue to write about issues I cared about, but I also wanted an editor. In hindsight, I think that

Salon was likely not the ideal place for my work, that it would have gotten more exposure (and I would have made a hell of a lot more money) if I'd just kept up the blog. I published the blog for only six weeks, and I was getting thousands of original hits a day.

Don't call me a blogger

But I'm not a blogger. I never wanted to be. I couldn't have blogged and also written the kind of ambitious fiction I was growing into writing. But, yes, from a purely pecuniary perspective, this was yet another missed opportunity by a Waldman— the way my parents waited to invest in silver until the night before the market crashed.

Writing about myself was personal right from the beginning. It was more terrifying than writing about anything else. And yet, one of the most unexpected things about writing memoir was that the disclosures that caused the most controversy were the ones I thought were pretty neutral.

The piece that caused the most controversy was definitely the one in the *New York Times*, the essay about loving my husband more than my kids. I'd actually written it for an anthology and had not submitted it to the *Times*. The editor of the Modern Love column found the essay on his own and asked me if he could reprint it. I was thrilled—I grew up in New Jersey and the *Times* was, in a sense, my hometown paper—but I had not really considered the implications of such a massive audience. The night before the piece was put to bed, I got a call saying the publisher was insisting that we pull the section about how Michael and I would go away and do Ecstasy together every few years. The editor suggested that we go to the mattresses to keep that piece of the story, but I told him that upon consideration, I didn't actually need the five million readers of the *New York Times* knowing that Michael and I did drugs together.

That was the only time I was ever censored. And the truth was, it was much for the best. Had that remained in the piece, it wouldn't have been as effective. Michael and I would have been dismissed as crazy people.

It's all about the voice

Personal essays are, for me, much easier to write than fiction. A novel is a much more serious endeavor for me. It tries to do a lot more. It takes much more focus. It's all about voice. Each novel requires a completely new voice, a compelling and fascinating voice, one that is distinct from my own. That takes tremendous focus to create and maintain. I don't always have the emotional fortitude to work on my novel. Writing a personal essay is like taking a break. I don't need to invent a voice. It's very easy for me to find my own. In some ways, even the most serious, painful essays write themselves.

The memoir of overprivilege

I'll always write essays, but I'm not sure I'll ever write another whole collection of them. I don't feel like I've had an interesting enough life for that. I'm always writing the book that I want to read, and who wants to read about a woman with a moderately successful though occasionally disappointing career, a great marriage, and some kids who have had challenges but are by and large lovely children? That shit is dull.

It's not that I'm saying that all memoir has to be Sturm und Drang. But the personal essay I hate most is what I call the essay of overprivilege—for example, the one about the trauma of first-class air travel. When I read that kind of essay I know that life has become too easy for that person. Something else has to happen for them to deserve to write a memoir. Some writers seem determined to limn the pleasures of life forever. I'm not one of them.

While I'm writing, I worry

While I'm writing, all I'm thinking about is the way the words sound, the way the sentences come out, and whether what I'm writing feels true. I never think about the reception the piece is going to get—never, ever, ever. Honestly, I wish I did. My life would be a lot easier.

Every once in a rare while I will think, Oh, God, what will my mother say? Then I tell myself to keep going, I can cut the offending bit out later on. In fact, I don't usually cut it; I just need that mantra to give myself permission to keep writing.

When I first started writing, Michael told me that if you're not uncomfortable, you're not writing what you need to write. If your work feels really safe and pleasant, there's a problem.

Writing memoir is the same in that way as writing fiction. Does the voice feel right? Are the characters doing what they would actually be doing? Have I spent enough time making sure the world I've created is real and true?

Whatever the genre, I'm always trying to write in a way that sounds good to the ear, that reads well, that will be meaningful to some group of people.

My biggest obstacle? Laziness

What gets in my way, more than anything, is my own laziness. I'd always rather surf the Web or lie around reading a novel than write. Kids, life, blah, blah, self-loathing—it all takes up so much time.

What do I worry about? I'm ashamed to say that what I worry about all too frequently is being respected. Will my literary idols, the writers whose work I respect and admire, look down their noses at me? Unfortunately, that happened a lot when I wrote the essay about loving my husband more than my kids. I was dismissed as a "women's writer." One who was interested in topics that weren't really serious. Topics like motherhood and relationships and life and death. You know, those silly girl things.

I try to protect my family. Sometimes I don't try hard enough.

The kids never asked me to stop writing about them. But when the older two reached a certain age, around bar mitzvah age—I figured if it's good enough for the Jews, it's good enough for me—I realized that they owned their own stories, and I wasn't entitled to use them anymore. So I stopped writing about them except with their specific permission.

Michael never had to ask me. He knows I'd never write anything negative about him. It wouldn't even occur to me to do that. Sometimes I read these really angry essays about someone's ongoing marriage, and I don't even understand the impulse to publish things like that. How do you do that and stay married?

Every once in a while, Michael has a problem with something I tweet. For example, this guy who hates my guts was trashing me on my Facebook page. The guy is a toxic, malevolent, misogynistic force on the Internet. I tweeted that he hates me because he wants to fuck my husband. The guy started threatening me. My response, as ever when I'm attacked, was "Bring it on, motherfucker. The truth is 100 percent protection against libel." Michael said to me, "Dude, I don't need this guy out there being angry. You dragged me into this." He asked me to apologize, and though I really didn't want to, I did. I tweeted that there were a myriad of reasons to loathe me other than wanting to fuck my husband, and that I owed this miscreant an apology for assuming I knew his motivation.

Otherwise, Michael never complains about anything I write. Sometimes I write about his dishwasher-loading skills, which leave much to be desired. That's about as bad as he's going to get from me.

Something I wrote in *Bad Mother* did cause a big problem for my son Zeke. I wrote that he once told us that he thought he might be gay, but that wasn't at all what bothered him. He's very secure in his sexuality. (He's straight, by the way.) It was that I wrote about breastfeeding him until he was nearly three years old that upset him. It never occurred to me that he'd be bothered by this. I mean, we live in Berkeley; there are probably fifth graders in his class still breastfeeding. There are probably kids whose earth mommies ship breast milk to them at college!

Though Zeke had cleared everything I wrote, after the book came out he was teased at school. They called him "Boob Boy," and he got really upset.

Another time, I had a really bad thing happen with one of my adult family members. I wrote something I shouldn't have, unintentionally insulting one of my siblings' children. I wouldn't have written it if I'd realized it was insulting, and I had the phrase taken out of the next printings of the book. But I lost my relationship with that sibling for years. It was horrible. It was one of the most unpleasant experiences of my life. He wasn't the only one who thought it was harsh. Other people were shocked, too. I never should have written it, and it's one of the biggest regrets of my life.

My best experience, writing memoir, was also my worst

The best experience I've had as a memoirist was also the worst experience. That first crazy essay about loving Michael more than my kids resulted in so much publicity, so much hate mail, and so many angry women confronting me on the set of *Oprah*. It was also the best experience, because it started a conversation that I believe had a part in changing how we talk about motherhood.

The incident was exciting in its way. I had never before experienced that kind of notoriety. To be recognized in the street was an unfamiliar sensation, as was hearing strangers who didn't recognize me talk about my work in front of me. There was a certain kind of thrill involved in that, but on the flip side, to be the target of so much anger was extraordinarily stressful.

When I opened my e-mail on the Sunday morning when my piece ran, I found hundreds and hundreds of e-mails. Page after page of e-mails, all from complete strangers. And the things people were writing! It was terrifying and awful. Some actually threatened me, told me I should "be shot," that I deserved to die. Someone actually taped a note to our gate that said, "Your children should be taken away from you."

It was frightening. But it was also kind of cool, since having people you don't respect hate you can actually be fun. If the editors of *Gawker* hate you, for example, it can be a sign that you're doing something right in the world.

And there's no denying that the whole adventure changed my career. If all I wanted to do for the rest of my life was to write personal essays, I'd be set. It just so happens that I also want to write serious literary fiction, which, given that the essay gave me the reputation for being a loudmouth, can be a challenge. There is certainly pressure on me to write more essays and another memoir, though to my publisher's credit that pressure doesn't come from them. They've been great about giving me lots of room to write what I want. But sometimes readers used to see my name and ask, "Isn't that the woman who exposes herself in print?" When *Love & Treasure* first came out, interviewers told me that they had a hard time believing that the same writer who wrote that essay also wrote a serious novel about the Holocaust.

The reviews of *Love & Treasure* have been so uniformly good, however, so serious and respectful, that I think that has changed things for me. I think the anxiety of not being respected has become less of a reality and more of a fear. It feels true, but only to me.

Social media eats novels alive

It's also possible the scandal helped my fiction career. Maybe it even brings me readers who wouldn't know me otherwise. It's hard to tell.

At same time, who the fuck knows *what* makes readers read certain books and ignore others? My publisher is delighted by my twelve thousand Twitter followers. But I'm not sure it matters at all. Following me on Twitter certainly doesn't mean that they'll buy my books. Some of them follow me because they heard I don't love my kids. Some because they like my serious fiction. Some because they agree with my politics. Some because the shit I say on Twitter scandalizes them and they enjoy being scandalized.

I sometimes worry that tweeting keeps my ideas from percolating into fully formed essays. When I have a thought or a feeling, instead of writing an essay about it, I shoot my wad on Twitter, and then—another great American memoir down the drain. (That comment was meant sarcastically, I hope you know.) If I didn't have fiction as a medium for deeper, more thoughtful expression, I'd stop the social media. I think.

Except that I have no choice but to admit that there's an exhibitionist quality to what I do on social media that satisfies some part of me that I'd just as soon deny exists. That deep, secret need is much easier to satisfy now that there's Twitter. But let's be clear, I'm not proud of the exhibitionist side of me. Maybe it's good that it's being forced into more narrow arenas. Maybe if social media means you need to have a really good reason to write a personal essay—like you need to pay your rent or your kid's tuition—it'll have a detrimental effect on personal writing that's motivated by that unpleasant impulse. Personal essays motivated by exhibitionist narcissism will vanish, leaving the field to those motivated by higher things. We can always dream.

But I don't mean to deny the delights of memoir writing. Writing a story that changes the way someone sees their life, or just gives them a sense of not being alone in the world, is incredibly satisfying. It can be deeply moving to know you've had a meaningful effect on someone's life. After I published the story of my abortion, I received an e-mail from a man who heard me being interviewed on NPR's *Fresh Air* as he and his wife were driving in the car. They were on their way home from the clinic, having had their own second-trimester abortion after a bad genetic diagnosis. He told me that they pulled over by the side of the road to listen. They sat in their car and cried. Before they heard me speak about it, they'd felt completely alone, as if they were the only people in the world who'd ever gone through a genetic termination.

That won't happen on Twitter. I can quip, I can rant, but I can't go deep on social media.

A memoir is not a diary

People want to believe that a memoirist has simply opened a vein and bled on the page. That's a diary, which can be emotionally satisfying, it can be great therapy, but it's not necessarily good writing. Writing memoir requires the construction of story and character in the same way that writing anything does. The trick with memoir is that the story and the character have to be true. Really true, not just emotionally "true." All memoirs, including mine, are made of constructed characters. By that I don't mean composites, but rather that every writer of memoir must choose what to say and how to say it, what parts of ourselves and others to reveal and what to hide. The story is personal and it's true and it's real, but it's also constructed.

The reader thinks they know all of you, but they know only the piece that you choose to reveal in the way you choose to reveal it. If you're doing your job, you're revealing your story and your characters thoughtfully and carefully. Maybe that's not a nice thing to think about when you're reading a memoir— that the author is conscious of how she's coming across, that she's presenting herself and her story with specificity and thoughtfulness. You're not just showing your best self—you're showing your honest self. But you don't owe your reader everything, every story of your life, every element of you. You owe your reader only what you want to reveal.

I like to think, and maybe I'm deluded in my thinking, that there's a point to writing honestly, but honesty doesn't demand completeness. You write honestly, but you're allowed to keep parts of yourself secret.

Personally, I have no problem with revealing truly ugly parts of my personality—almost to a fault. I'm always ready to reveal the most hideous things. Sometimes when I have a good editor she'll say, "You don't have to put it like *that*. Why show your *worst* self on the page, when there's always those other elements that are far more flattering?" My best editors demand that I show my whole self, not just my icky bits. They insist that I not only indulge my self-loathing but also be willing to be positive. That's so much harder for me.

The secrets I hold back are about my family members. But

every writer has her own secret places and things she holds back.

Of course, my saying that makes you want to know exactly what those secrets are—doesn't it?

Ayelet Waldman's Wisdom for Memoir Writers

- If you're not uncomfortable and scared while you're writing, you're not writing close enough to the bone.
- Writing is a discipline. Don't wait for the muse to show up; if you do, you'll discover that she's gone over to someone else's desk.
- If you're afraid of whatever you're writing, just tell yourself you can cut it later, and keep on writing.

Chapter Nineteen

Jesmyn Ward

Whenever my mother drove us from coastal Mississippi to New Orleans to visit my father on the weekend, she would say, "Lock the doors." After my mother and father split for the last time before they divorced, my father moved to New Orleans, while we remained in DeLisle, Mississippi.

—Opening, *Men We Reaped*, 2013

We live in a nation that loves a rags-to-riches bootstrap story, and no wonder: the myth that "anyone can make it in America" is, paradoxically, an effective tool for keeping gender, class, and racial inequities in place.

Jesmyn Ward embodies the bootstrap narrative, even as the content and intent of her work rips that myth into shreds. Born poor and black in rural DeLisle, Mississippi, she was raised on food stamps. Her mother was a maid; her father worked a variety of blue-collar jobs. He fought dogs for sport and eventually left the family. Jesmyn went to private school, where she was bullied for being the only black girl, her tuition paid by one of her mother's employers.

In 2005 Jesmyn earned her MFA in creative writing at the University of Michigan, where she wrote her first novel, *Where the Line Bleeds*, about a struggling family in a rural Gulf Coast town. Later that year, she and her family were devastated by Hurricane Katrina: their home flooded, possessions destroyed, stranded in their car in a field. After the storm, Jesmyn took a job at the University of New Orleans. She didn't write anything during the three years following Katrina.

Her second novel, *Salvage the Bones*, takes place over twelve days before, during, and after Hurricane Katrina. On November 16, 2011, the novel won the National Book Award for Fiction, bringing the girl from DeLisle to international prominence. "I wanted to write about the experiences of the poor and the black and the rural people of the South," she told the audience, "so that the culture that marginalized us for so long would see that our stories were as universal, our lives as fraught and lovely and important as theirs."

Next came the memoir *Men We Reaped*, sparked by the premature deaths of her brother and four other young African American men in DeLisle. "I fought against writing this memoir for a long time," Jesmyn said. "I knew that I had a story to tell, but I lacked emotional distance on those deaths . . . I had to deal with my own guilt and a sense of worthlessness that no amount of scholarships and awards could cancel out."

THE VITALS

Birthday: April 1977

Born and raised: DeLisle, Mississippi

Home now: New Orleans, Louisiana

Family: Daughter, age two

Schooling: BA and master's degree, Stanford University; MFA, University of Michigan

Day job: Teaching creative writing at Tulane University

Notable notes:
- Jesmyn has her deceased brother's signature tattooed on her left wrist and the words "Love brother" on her right.
- Jesmyn was a Stegner Fellow at Stanford from 2008 to 2010.
- Jesmyn's *Salvage the Bones* won the 2011 National Book Award for Fiction and a 2012 Alex Award.

Facebook: https://www.facebook.com/pages/Jesmyn-Ward/110681739048514?fref=ts

Twitter: @jesmimi

Website: jesmimi.blogspot.com

THE COLLECTED WORKS

Memoir

Men We Reaped, 2013

Novels

Where the Line Bleeds, 2008

Salvage the Bones, 2011

Jesmyn Ward

Why I write about myself

By the time I wrote my memoir, *Men We Reaped*, I had been running from writing it for a long time. When the events in the book were happening, I knew I'd probably write about them one day. I didn't want to. I'd studied fiction, and I was committed to establishing myself as a fiction writer first.

I knew it would be painful to write a memoir. I didn't feel equipped for that. I knew you needed to open yourself and be vulnerable. I was not ready for that.

I fought it for a long time. Then in 2009, I finished the last draft of *Salvage* and I wanted to work on a first draft of something new. I kept writing the first chapter of a new novel over and over. It wasn't working. I thought maybe I was supposed to be writing something else.

I began thinking about what had happened to my brother, and to my friends. My brother died in 2000. Between then and 2004, four of my friends died. I was like a wounded animal while all that death was happening. Eventually, enough years had passed that I began to think about what that story would be like on the page, how I'd tell that story. I needed that time to gain some distance, to begin to see it and process it as a story.

This was when I was at Stanford as a Stegner Fellow. My friends were smart, well-read people, and they were all great writers, and when I told them my story, they all encouraged me to write a memoir. They said it would make a great memoir, and they said it was a story people needed to read. They felt it could have a real impact.

I know it sounds crazy, but I hadn't really thought about what telling my story could do. I was so terrified of doing it that I didn't want to think about how it would be received. Once these people I respected told me that people needed to read it, then I could start.

Every time I considered what this story could do for some kid who lives out in the plains of Nebraska, growing up in a neighborhood where there's drug addiction, where there are people dying young, I thought that if I'd had a book like that, it wouldn't have made the pain bearable, but it might have made it so that I was able to continue. Holding the realization of what this story could do for a kid like me who's young now, and lives in the rural South, and might be losing people—holding that close to me when I felt like I was breaking every day—reaffirmed the importance of doing it.

Writing the memoir broke me

Writing *Men We Reaped* broke me in different ways at different spots in the drafting process. The first draft was hard because I was just getting it out. In some ways, that draft failed. I was really just telling the story, not making assessments this happened, then this. Just putting those facts down on paper was really painful. There were moments when I'd stop typing, sit there and read what I wrote, and think, I can't believe I just wrote this.

A lot of the time when I was writing about my mom, who's a very private person, I felt like I was betraying her. Or when I was writing very personal things about my own experience, I'd stop and say, Am I really going to do this?

The further I got into the book, the worse it got. Recounting the events when my brother died was so difficult. The edits, especially the very big edit I did with the direction of my editor, Kathy Belden, was one of the hardest things I've ever done in relation to writing. I did four drafts, and she was asking me at every point to offer some judgment, some assessment of these events.

I'd been in therapy before. But the therapeutic work I did, writing the memoir, was exactly the kind of work I needed to do. I tackled those issues with Kathy Belden. I trusted Kathy when we were working on *Salvage the Bones*, but our relationship really deepened on *Men We Reaped*.

In the section about growing up in a seedy subdivision, I recounted a story about a cellar in the woods. Kathy had a page of notes on that section. She kept telling me to dig deeper, to look at myself in the past, to figure out why that cellar meant something to me.

Working through that chapter, I finally realized what that cellar had taken on for me. All the feelings of self-loathing and worthlessness I had at that age were embodied by that cellar. It symbolized all the dark things that happened to me, things I thought I deserved because of the way I thought of myself at that time: as a young black woman in the South. My ideas about sexuality, gender, romantic relationships—all my nebulous ideas about myself, and who I'd grow up to be, were all tied into that cellar. I didn't realize any of that until I was working on revisions.

When I did realize it, I also realized how much I was formed by what my mother and father were going through, and what the culture at large thought I was worth. Of course at that time I couldn't articulate any of that. But in that moment of revision, suddenly everything became very clear to me: the magnitude of my self-loathing, the magnitude of that larger culture, the system that told me I was nothing. Suddenly all of that was very clear. It broke something in me to realize how helpless I was in the face of all that.

People ask me if I think I'll write another memoir. I always say no. The process of writing the first one was so awful, I don't know if I could do it again.

It broke my mother, too

I was afraid while I was writing the memoir that my mother would disown me. She didn't, which was great, because that was my biggest fear. I don't know what I'd do without my family.

But my mother didn't like the book. It's so personal for her. She couldn't see what I was attempting to do. I wrote the memoir as a love letter to our family. She read it as a condemnation. All she saw was herself on the page. She said, "Please don't write about me again while I'm alive. It's okay when I'm gone." I told her I wouldn't.

My mom has always been a very private person. In her parenting style, she's authoritative. It's hard for her to open up, I guess. She had such a hard childhood and such a hard life in general. Her young adult years were difficult for her.

We love each other, and our relationship isn't easy. I've met women who come to their adulthood, and their mothers are still their mothers, but there's relaxed, affectionate camaraderie between them. My mother and I have never had that kind of relationship, and I don't think we ever will.

She let it be known she was displeased with the book. She didn't want to talk about it with me. She kept putting it off. When we finally talked about it, it was a difficult conversation, and not a very successful one. It felt like we were talking past each other.

We're still talking, and we still have the relationship we

had before, but it was bumpy for a while. That's another reason I don't know if I'll write another memoir.

Other relationships got better

On the whole, the memoir strengthened my relationships with other people: the cousins of the young men I wrote about, my sisters, my friends. My truths regarding what happened, the story I saw and understand and told, aligned closely with what they experienced. There was no dispute there.

They knew I was working on the book. I came to them for my research. I asked them lots of questions. For the cousins of the young men and for my sisters and friends, it was a much more active, participatory process than it was for my mother. They felt it was their book, too. They gave me the bulk of the information that I needed to write the sections about the young men who died.

That wasn't true with the families of the young men who died. I didn't speak to their mothers. In some cases I didn't speak to their siblings. There's this culture around death—specifically, around young people dying in the rural South: When someone young dies, they have these T-shirts with pictures on them of the deceased. On the T-shirts you can tell the date when they died. It's almost like they're made into saints.

That happened with my own brother. There's nothing wrong with it; it's a natural reaction, a part of grieving. But it makes writing a memoir problematic, because that desire for the deceased to be perfect, the angel, is still there. It's hard for immediate family members to see them as human, fallible. I would have been writing against that idealization if I had relied for the bulk of my research on the family members. So I avoided talking to them.

I knew, too, that they would put some pressure on me when the book came out. They'd look at the book and say, "This isn't what I told her." But I was writing a memoir. I wanted it to align with my truth as closely as it could. My experience of knowing the young men—that's the story.

The cousins I spoke to, they were there when I was there. We were all out doing the same things together, out at the club, staying up all night, getting high, all those things I write about. We were young and dumb together. But I wasn't there all the time. I went off to school. I wasn't there for much of what they were doing with the young men who died. So I asked them to tell me about the conversations they had with them: what were they thinking about, what were they struggling with?

Writing about a problem shouldn't make the problem worse

When I was writing my first novel, which had young black men as its main characters, I was very invested in telling the story, and also very worried about the effects the story would have.

I was worried that what I was writing would reinforce stereotypes, rather than break or confront them. I was worried about that a bit with *Salvage the Bones*, but not as much. I was a little older when I wrote *Salvage*, and writing the first novel had taught me some things. With the second novel I was confident enough to let the story come alive, to have a life of its own. The characters felt very human to me, so I was less worried about reinforcing stereotypes. The characters were strong enough to counteract any stereotypical ideas that readers coming into the book might have had.

With memoir, you have to tell the truth, right? I knew that the truth might be problematic for some people because in this country, unfortunately, the dialogue about black people seems to revolve around racist ideas. It's all about blaming African Americans. It's all about the individual being at fault—for our own ineptitude, our own defects. There's no awareness of the larger systematic pressures that bear down on us that make it easier for the sort of reality I write about to exist.

So my main concern with the memoir was giving that context to the reader, making those connections for the reader, bringing the larger picture back to the reader, giving the reader a rubric for understanding the individual stories. In the end I hoped that if I told the truth as I understood it about those systematic pressures, and how they affect individual actions and reactions, that would counteract any racist or narrow ideas people had about African American people acting badly.

Best-case scenario: memoir helps

Part of the reason I was so committed to telling this story was that there were other people out there living through this who were wondering why nothing of their experience was being reflected back to them in the media, TV, books, anything. They can't see themselves in the outside world. I wanted this book to reach them.

At the same time, I hoped this book might entice white people who wouldn't have read my book before I won that award. I wanted to make those connections for them, to help them see us in a way they'd never seen us before, and understand us the way they hadn't before.

I think it's working. On book tour I meet a lot of people from totally different backgrounds who find something in the memoir that resonates with them. Sometimes that means they read the book, and they do see us as human beings. Sometimes the connection point has less to do with race than grief and loss. For some people who are very different from me, that's what they take from it. That's fine. That's great. It's something we all share: loss, grief.

Winning the National Book Award

Winning the award expanded my audience. It made me aware of how important the memoir would be, and why I had to get it right. I was given the opportunity to say something that on the whole people haven't heard, something many writers want to say but haven't had the opportunity to say. I knew I had this one chance, and I had to take advantage of it. I felt an added pressure because of that.

Learning on the job

I'm trained as a fiction writer. I've taken only one creative nonfiction class. And yet I did it—I wrote a memoir. I think it might surprise my readers to know that, for those like me who want to write a memoir but don't have any background in creative nonfiction, if you've done the work to become a better writer, a better storyteller, that understanding serves you well when you're writing a memoir.

Jesmyn Ward's Wisdom for Memoir Writers

- Unlike with fiction, it's easiest to write a memoir from an outline. You have your experience and your truth to draw from, but there's so much there. You're whittling away at your life to find the story underneath. An outline helps.

- You get the most powerful material when you write toward whatever hurts. Don't avoid it. Don't run from it. Don't write toward what's easy. We recognize our humanity in those most difficult moments that people share.

- Whatever kind of writing you've done will help you write a memoir. If you've done that work, you have those tools, and you bring them to the work. They lead you. They guide you. They inform you when you're writing.

CHAPTER TWENTY

Edmund White

*I discovered France through Marie-Claude de Brunhoff. I'd
met her at a party in New York around 1975 and I'd been
struck right away by how polished and elegant she was.
Marie-Claude gleamed like the inside of a nautilus shell. She
wasn't tall, but she held herself as if she were.*

—Opening, *Inside a Pearl*, 2014

Despite exaggerated rumors of our "postracial," "postmi-
sogynistic," "posthomophobic" society, this stubborn fact
persists: American writers who are not white males are assigned
a literary identity based on their "otherness," whether they want
it or not.

Just as Jesmyn Ward is labeled an "African American
writer" and Cheryl Strayed's *Wild* might have been positioned
entirely differently had it been *Wild Man*, Edmund White's
sexual orientation, subject matter, and AIDS activism have
earned him the label "gay writer."

The moniker is not without basis. In the early 1980s, Ed-
mund and six other gay New York writers—Andrew Holleran,
Robert Ferro, Felice Picano, George Whitmore, Christopher
Cox, and Michael Grumley—formed a writing group they

called "the Violet Quill" to support one another's contributions to the emerging gay culture. A few years after the 1977 publication of his best-known nonfiction book, *The Joy of Gay Sex*, Edmund cofounded New York's Gay Men's Health Crisis, the first AIDS advocacy group in the country.

Over the next decade or so he published *A Boy's Own Story*, the first in his series of "autobiographical fiction," and *The Beautiful Room Is Empty*, the second. With *The Farewell Symphony*, published in 1997, Edmund White provided a fully formed portrait of a gay man in America, from coming out to middle age.

In a 1991 essay, "Out of the Closet, Onto the Bookshelf," White wrote, "As a young teen-ager I looked desperately for things to read that might excite me or assure me I wasn't the only one, that might confirm an identity I was unhappily piecing together."

"White is an acclaimed novelist, essayist, biographer of Genet and Proust, and a self-described 'archaeologist of gossip,'" a reviewer for *Booklist* wrote in 2013. "For White, identity is sexual identity . . . his principal concerns are fame, money, and, yes, sex."

THE VITALS

Birthday: January 13, 1940

Born and raised: Cincinnati, Ohio

Home now: New York, New York

Family: Married to Michael Carroll

Schooling: Cranbrook Schools, Bloomfield Hills, Michigan; University of Michigan

Day job: Professor of creative writing at Princeton University

Notable notes:
- As an undergraduate, Edmund studied Chinese. He was accepted into Harvard's Chinese doctoral program but followed a lover to New York instead.
- Before he became a full-time writer, Edmund White worked for Time-Life Books, *Newsweek*, *Saturday Review*, and *The New Republic*.
- Edmund White is a member of the American Academy of Arts and Letters, received a Guggenheim Fellowship in 1983, and won the National Book Critics Circle Award in 1994.

Facebook: https://www.facebook.com/edmund.white.12?fref=ts

Website: www.edmundwhite.com

THE COLLECTED WORKS

Memoirs/ Autobiographical Novels

A Boy's Own Story, 1982

The Beautiful Room Is Empty, 1988

My Lives, 2006

City Boy, 2009

Inside a Pearl, 2014

Plays

Terre Haute, 2006

Novels

Forgetting Elena, 1973

Nocturnes for the King of Naples, 1978

Caracole, 1985

The Farewell Symphony, 1997

The Married Man, 2000

Fanny, 2003

Chaos, 2007

Hotel de Dream, 2007

Jack Holmes and His Friend, 2012

Short Stories

Skinned Alive, 1995

Nonfiction

The Joy of Gay Sex (coauthored
with Charles Silverstein),
1977

States of Desire, 1980

The Darker Proof, 1988

Genet: A Biography, 1993

The Burning Library, 1994

Our Paris, 1994

Marcel Proust, 1999

Loss within Loss, 2001

The Flâneur, 2001

Arts and Letters, 2004

Rimbaud, 2008

Sacred Monsters, 2011

Edmund White

Why I write about myself

I hate the phrase "creative nonfiction." It sounds like a synonym for lying. You have to tell the truth when you're writing what purports to be a memoir.

I started off writing autobiographical fiction with my third novel, *A Boy's Own Story*. That was in 1982. In those days, normal people like me couldn't write memoirs. You had to be the hero of Iwo Jima or something. The story of someone who'd merely lived and suffered wasn't sensational enough.

I moved to Paris in 1983. While I was living there, the "normal person memoir" fad began to catch on in the States. Usually the author was someone with a painful childhood, like Mary Karr. I remember coming back to America on holiday and seeing an ad in *The New York Review of Books* that said, "Have you been raped as a child? Incested? We can put you on the lecture circuit." That's how I knew that memoir was in.

I called *A Boy's Own Story* and *Beautiful Room* "novels." And indeed they were. I thought I could redress the balance between truth and invention by calling them novels. I think fiction should be representative, and memoir should be extremely honest and personal. It should show the author for who he is, warts and all.

The memoirist's contract

The opposite of an autobiographical novel is a novelistic memoir. Unless they're written for humorous effect, like the work of David Sedaris, they're reprehensible.

A memoirist's contract with the reader is that you're telling the truth and nothing but the truth. Maybe I think that because I do both. For me it's been interesting to write about the same episodes in my life in both fiction and nonfiction forms and try to make them not repetitious. For instance, in *My Lives* I tried not to write at all about my childhood. I tried not to write at all chronologically, but by topic. The chapters were "My Blonds," "My Shrinks," et cetera. The structure was almost an essayistic sort.

Another distinction is that with fiction, you cannot have opinions about things. You present the action, the dialogue. You don't say, "She's a good person," or "That was a formative experience." Only bad novels are explicit like that. People can draw that information themselves from a good novel.

When you write a memoir about the five shrinks you had

over twenty-five years, you're almost obliged at the end of it to say if they were positive or negative, and what it did for and against you. You have to have an opinion. I'm writing a novel now about a male model who comes from France to America in 1980, just when models became supermodels. I want to show that he's like a black hole in space. He doesn't have that many characteristics, so everyone projects onto him. In a memoir I'd say, "I knew a model. Everyone would project on him. They'd attribute characteristics to him. They made him into the image of what they wanted him to be."

In a novel, you'd dramatize that in a way that assumes the reader is attentive and can think for himself. I'd have another character attribute bad things to my model, in hopes the reader will realize these aren't based on actual characteristics, but on their projections—which say more about the speaker than the one he's speaking of.

No detail is too strange for a memoir

The fiction writer's job is to turn out a manuscript that is well shaped, that has a beginning, a middle, and an end, and is fairly suspenseful and whose characters behave in a fairly coherent, believable way. Those demands are higher in fiction than in nonfiction.

I have a friend, an Englishwoman, who insists on calling her memoirs "novels." Yet there are all these kind of screwy things in them that wouldn't be explicable in fiction. She'll talk about how some man slapped some other man on the back, and something flew out of his mouth and across the room. What was it? Teeth? Food? She'll say, "I don't know, but it really happened."

You can get away with that in a memoir, but not in a novel. Details that are very strange, that don't pay off—you can introduce them into a memoir, because they were very striking at the time, and they really happened to you. In a novel they have to pay off.

The fictional contract

A novelist has a different contract with the reader than a memoirist. Novels are more work for the reader. The novel is meant to be a normalized, representative version of the class of person the author is writing about.

Here's a recent example. I reviewed Francine Prose's new book on the front page of *The New York Times Book Review*. I had one complaint about the book, which was that Prose made the lesbian cross-dresser a Nazi. If you're writing a biography of a real-life person who's a lesbian and a Nazi, you'd be justified. But in a novel, when you have only one lesbian character, to make her a spy and a complete nut is offensive. I say that not out of any rigorous sense of political correctness, but because that character isn't representative or normalizing of lesbians.

In her novels, Jane Austen writes about young, oftentimes poor gentry women who make advantageous marriages in spite of their ridiculous fathers or mothers. Her heroines are attractive and representative of that segment of their demographic of their times. In real life, Jane Austen never got married, had to hide from her family that she was a writer, and slept on a couch in the living room. If she had written an autobiography, it would have seemed very weird to most people.

I know that mine is an extreme view. In *A Passage to India,*

E. M. Forster altogether leaves out his own homosexuality. He did write a gay novel, but he didn't allow it to be published until after his death.

Proust is another case. In *Remembrance of Things Past*, almost all of the characters are gay. But the narrator, who is called Marcel, is not gay, and he's also not Jewish, as Proust actually was. In other words, he's sort of normalized in that he's straight and Catholic. The bizarre aspects of his own life are completely suppressed. Proust never wrote a real autobiography, though in letters he sometimes referred to his novel as a memoir. It obviously wasn't. Almost everything was changed. He changed men into women, and he made himself into a good Catholic.

My protagonist in *A Boy's Own Story* was much less precocious intellectually and sexually than I was. He was shyer. If I'd written about myself as the freaky boy I really was, very few people could have identified with that novel. That book came out in '82. I don't think that was quite the period yet for my own true story. In real life, I had had sex with five hundred men, most of them older than I was, by the time I was sixteen. The boy in the book has one or two experiences, with boys his own age.

I made several efforts to make the boy in *Boy's* relatable. I didn't name the decade he was growing up in. I didn't name the place. I didn't give him a name. Not a week goes by that I don't get a letter about that book from someone like the sixteen-year-old gay black guy from Ghana, who wrote me last, "My life is exactly like yours." It's kind of crazy that a sixteen-year-old gay black guy from Ghana thinks his life is like a white boy's in the Midwest. By taking away the name of the decade, the name of the place, and his name, I kind of made my protagonist like every boy.

My readers and me

When you write memoir, the voice is very important. It needs to be very companionable for the reader. I always have a tough time, because I'm aware of writing for many middle-aged, middle-class women, and I'm writing about something most women don't like at all: male homosexuality. They're offended by it. It doesn't interest them. Maybe they find it abhorrent. Straight men are turned on by lesbians, whereas straight women—unless they're young and kinky—are not turned on by gay men.

I know teenage girls who watch gay male porn. The barrier between lesbian women and heterosexuality is much more permeable than it is for men. Years ago *Playboy* had a quiz in which they asked, "What's your most exciting forbidden fantasy?" Fifty percent of women said they wanted to try lesbianism. Only 3 percent of men wanted to try sex with another man. It has to do with the sexist nature of our culture. Men are taken much more seriously. So I have to try to place my experiences in a perspective that's more general, told in a voice that's kind of sympathetic and brotherly.

Truth, lies, and memoir

I just published a memoir about my years in Paris. A French friend of mine—an ex-lover, actually—read it and was very shocked that I left out a girlfriend of mine and his. According to him, she'd played such an important role in my life.

My friend was complaining about lots of things in the book. "In the memoir," he said, "you're so cruel and harsh. In real life I know you're a kind person, very patient and good natured and nonjudgmental. In your memoir you're very *dur*— very hard."

This story is a perfect example of the difference between memoir and fiction. In a memoir I could say that this friend of mine, with all his criticisms of my "hardness," was a pathological liar. He claimed his family was aristocratic, that his mother committed suicide, that she was a concert pianist. I knew his mother was a hairdresser who played accordion. He said his grandmother wouldn't meet me because she was Catholic and hated homosexuals. I met his grandmother at his funeral. She was very bawdy, with lots of lovers in her seventies, completely different from how he'd described her. The guy didn't lie to get ahead; he just wanted to sound more interesting than he was.

When I wrote about this guy in a novel, in order to add suspense, the narrator didn't discover these lies until after the ex-lover was dead.

There have been so many scandals about memoirs that weren't true. The author of *Midnight in the Garden of Good and Evil* confessed that he'd taken two phone conversations that were crucial to the story and collapsed them into one. People were very disturbed when the author of *A Million Little Pieces*, which purported to be a memoir and was directed to a very vulnerable population of recovering addicts, admitted that his girlfriend hadn't really committed suicide. There were some other very important events that he falsified, which led to his denunciation on *Oprah*.

That's a good example to keep in mind. People do feel cheated when you lie in a memoir because you've broken your contract with your readers.

The long arm of the law

With my most recent memoir, and with all my memoirs, I worked a lot with lawyers. I had to make 74 changes for the American lawyer. For the British edition, I had to make 134 changes. For example, I told a story in the memoir about an Englishwoman friend who came to Paris to visit me with her younger husband. At the time I was going out with a male model who was about twenty and incredibly beautiful. Her husband fell in love with this twenty-year-old boy. He was ogling and drooling.

I didn't think that was something to be challenged, but the British lawyer said to take it out and I did. In America it's been established by law that it's not actionable to call someone gay even if they're heterosexual, because it's no longer considered prejudicial. Apparently that's not true in Britain, and I didn't want to be the test case.

Write a little memoir, do a little damage

I have an ex-lover who's Swiss. I haven't heard from him since my memoir came out. I think the portrait I did of him is very loving, very fair. He might feel it's too revealing. I wrote to a mutual friend of ours, saying, I haven't heard from Mateus, is he pissed off at me or what? I haven't heard back.

In general, I try to be very honest in my memoirs. If I lose the friendship, so what? I believe Milosz, the Nobel-winning Polish poet, who said, "Whenever a writer is born into a family, that family is destroyed."

On the other hand I sometimes say the best way to keep a secret is to publish it, since no one reads. My books aren't indexed. So anyone who wants to know what I wrote about him has to read the whole thing.

Edmund White's Wisdom for Memoir Writers

- Cut to the chase. Don't burden yourself with lots of exposition. What you imagine is the connective tissue can oftentimes be dropped. See if maybe a phrase or two can do it.

- You can foreshorten lots of boring dialogue by paraphrasing: "She told me the story of her marriage." Sedaris will have conversations between his six-year-old self and his mother, and it's funny, but it isn't very plausible that he'd remember what he said when he was six. I buy it only because it's funny, and an important plot point isn't hanging on it.

- Sit in a café by yourself, and listen to the people in the next booth. You're clear about what's going on. You know they're fighting about sex, or fidelity, or money. You don't know who Martha is, but you get it. Apply that to your writing.

- Use some novelistic techniques so you don't just have voices talking in the dark. Make your reader see and smell and feel things by using sensual details.